HEALING ENERGY

The Power of Recovery

Ruth Fishel, M.Ed., C.A.C.

Health Communications, Inc.
Deerfield Beach, Florida

Ruth Fishel
Spirithaven
1600 Falmouth Road, Suite 175-1980
Centerville, MA 02632

Library of Congress Cataloging-in-Publication Data

Fishel, Ruth
Healing energy: the power of recovery / Ruth Fishel.
p. cm.
Includes bibliographical references.
ISBN 1-55874-128-3
1. Narcotic addicts — Rehabilitation. 2. Self-care, Health.
I. Title.
RC564.29.F58 1991 90-20544
616.86'06—dc20 CIP

ISBN 1-55874-128-3

Publisher: Health Communications, Inc.
3201 S.W. 15th Street
Deerfield Beach, Florida 33442-8190

Cover design by Iris T. Slones

DEDICATION

To Stephen, Don and Paul and all the other gentle and beautiful men, women and children who have died of AIDS. So many times you held me up in my own recovery. You died much too early and I miss you.

May your light shine so brightly on our planet that all people can see that the destructive barriers of race, color, creed, religion and sex, or sexuality, are merely human-made illusions.

And may all these artificial walls that are destroying our lives and our planet . . .

. . . soon come tumbling down.

Acknowledgments

This book is actually a synthesis of all the books that I have read, all the conferences and lectures that I have attended, and all the people with whom I have spoken, worked with and learned from over many years. It could not have been written without the research and reporting of thousands of scientists, writers, educators and spiritual leaders and I acknowledge with deep gratitude all who have listened to their calling to work for the betterment of humanity.

Tremendous advances have taken place in the mind/body/spirit field in this past decade and are still continuing to be made. The new found science of psychoneuroimmunology, or PSI, has proven medically both the positive and negative connection between our minds, bodies and immune systems. The devastating disease of AIDS has accelerated scientific and medical research in the areas of our immune system.

The world is reaching a higher level of consciousness and of mental, physical and spiritual health due to, in a large degree, the work of Bill Wilson and Dr. Bob Smith, co-founders in 1935 of Alcoholics Anonymous and the Twelve-Step movement. I owe not only this book but my life to the principles of the movement that they have left to the world. The extraordinary changes that have taken place in the governments and thus the lives of the people in Europe and Asia and Africa are the direct results of the changes that are taking place in more and more individuals at a deeper personal level.

Meditation was the connection that I found so exciting. It moved me deeply (actually pushed me) to bring what I was learning to the field of recovery. Meditation bathed its light on my own personal path of recovery and made a very clear and simple bridge between some of the East and West thinking, science and medicine, psychotherapy, spirituality, and the 12 Steps of recovery.

I am also deeply grateful to:

- Insight meditation teachers Larry Rosenberg, Sharon Salzberg, Joseph Goldstein and Jack Kornfield, for their retreats, tapes, books, articles and classes. They have helped me to open my heart and have moved me to pass on what I have found.
- Everyone at Health Communications and U.S. Journal, especially to Peter Vegso and Gary Seidler, founders and owners, for continuing to believe in me. They were among the very first in the field of recovery to take risks in the publishing and conference world, and I honor their courage, foresight and perseverance. The wonderful staff including Reta, Suzanne, Vicky, LuAnn, Milena, Michael, Randy and Teri have always been there for me in the most supportive ways.
- Marie Stilkind, my editor at Health Communications, who always has the right word to encourage me or to make me laugh, who believes in me and has become a very dear friend over the years of our working together over 1800 miles of telephone wires; and who has a magical way of taking my manuscripts and notes, additions and corrections, and making them come out looking like a real book.
- My parents, who did their very best to bring to my life what they thought would make me happy. They gave me what they had so I could climb to the next step on the ladder of human evolution. I struggled deeply about whether to share some of the painful events in my books, even up to the time that I saw my words in typeset. But these events have been part of my journey and my intent is to share my own experience, strength and hope with you, the reader.
- To friends like Diane Crosby, Ellen Harris, Joy Miller, Gina Ogden, Sandy Siraco, Rosalie Smith, Barbara Thomas and Eileen White, who believe in me and encourage me when

I need it the most, and to Maureen Lydon who is no longer with us and who I miss very much.

- To my new friends on Cape Cod who have made me feel at home and loved and part of their family.
- To my wonderful adult kids: Debbie Boisseau, Bob Fishel and Judy Fishel who have more than tolerated me in my unique, not so ordinary journey. Today I always feel their love, their respect, their encouragement and understanding and for this I am so deeply grateful!
- To Sandy Bierig, my partner, life-traveling companion and the first person who sees my written words hot off the computer. She tolerates me through all the mood changes I go through in my creative process, adds clarity, insight, encouragement, truth, love and proper English where it is most needed.
- And to all the courageous people in recovery who continue to pass it on!

God bless you all!

In Peace and Love,
Ruth
Cape Cod

CONTENTS

PART ONE

We must understand that all personal growth is intended for the awakening of the whole.

Richard Moss

1

Awakening To Healing And Recovery

It is as if a river that had run to waste
in sluggish side-streams and marshes
suddenly found its way back to its proper bed,
or as if a stone lying on a germinating seed
were lifted away so that the shoot
could begin its natural growth.

Carl Jung

On a recent trip I received the gift of witnessing the healing powers of nature at its most basic, fundamental and natural level. I drove through Mount St. Helens in Washington State nine years after the devastating volcano had erupted its destructive ash down the mountainside, killing everything in its path. All the trees for miles around the mouth of the volcano had fallen like match sticks. They looked like thousands and thousands of telephone poles fallen in straight rows along the mountain side. Gray ash still covered everything, and it looked as if a major war had been fought and lost. It was an awesome sight. The destructive power of nature could not be denied.

My partner and I stopped by the side of the road to rest and take pictures. Our mood was heavy and full of awe. An enormous sense of loss began to envelop us. I had a new respect for a force far greater than my understanding.

On this day the sun was shining brightly; the sky a clear and beautiful blue in sharp contrast to the sights on the mountain. Looking down I was startled to see a small ant slowly making its way across the ground. As my eyes followed the ant's progress, I smiled to discover a green leaf pushing up from the ash-covered ground. And a few yards further a purple flower was in bloom.

In the silence that seemed to fill the entire universe an unexpected and exquisite song from an unseen bird filled that silent space and my eyes were suddenly full of tears.

Life was going on. In the midst of all the ravages of this natural destruction, Mother Nature was alive and well. It was as if she had been sleeping, resting and growing stronger all the time and was now ready to burst forth in a glorious rebirth.

A short time later we traveled through Yellowstone National Park. It was just one year after the worst fire in its history had destroyed a large area of trees and foliage. Many animals had been killed in this "human-made" disaster, suspected to have been started by a carelessly discarded match. Healthy rich green forests lived side by side with blackened trunks and bare branches. Beautiful deer bounded by. Antelopes, black bears, buffalo, coyotes and many other animals still flourished in the woods that had been untouched by the fire.

In the fire-destroyed forest here and there a new flower or leaf had begun its miraculous struggle to push its way up through the charred ground.

Another rebirth! A celebration of Life! The Mysterious Powers and Energies of the universe continued to unfold in the natural process of life and death, teaching new lessons in faith and trust for those of us who want to look.

So many of us have experienced our own devastation, our own volcanoes, our own natural and self-made disasters. We have struggled from birth, attempting to flower and grow in homes full of fire and ashes, sickness and ignorance, dysfunction and addiction, alcoholism and drugs, fear and violence. We have suffered to survive and to find reason and purpose in our lives.

Somewhere within all of us we caught sight of enough sunlight, were touched by enough love and, whether we knew it consciously or not, we felt there just be a Higher Presence, a Spirit, a Power Greater than ourselves, so we hung in there. We could not give up. Even in our deepest, darkest times of pain and suffering we still reached up. We still accepted. However hesitantly or skeptically, we took the hand that was extended to us.

We survived!

Each and every one of us is a very special and important human being, with gifts and talents still unknown, still untapped within us, just waiting to be discovered. We have ached from a place so deep within to know who we are, to know what life is all about.

Some of us thought we had the answers and pursued our paths, only to find out that we came to dead ends or detours. Some of us had a particular strength or quality that enabled us to reach that detour and look around the corner for another road. Others reached out for help and found it. And still others came to a dead stop, not knowing what to do with their pain.

Many stopped trying.

Many of those who stopped trying are not alive today.

Many human beings are still in great pain.

Many are in denial.

But more and more people today are in recovery.

Some people have been fortunate enough to have recovered their power, discovered and developed their gifts and are right now at this very moment sharing their gifts with the world. At first this recovery began with just two people, then a few more. Today their numbers are rapidly increasing because of a movement that began in 1935 and has spread its arms to join and heal people all over the world.

For those of us who are already in recovery, we have been gifted with very special steps. These gifts that have turned our lives around actually have the ability to help change the universe from a place of war, starvation, cruelty, poverty, prejudice, lies, denial, misused power, disease and suffering, to a place of peace and love.

We have the opportunity to merge our energies with the energies of others who are also growing in numbers and influence every day.

We all have access to the power to change ourselves. And, contrary to popular opinion, I believe this change brings change to others. Each affects what is going on around us in some way.

I believe that the change that we are making is powerful enough to ultimately change the universe.

We cannot make others change the way we want them to change. But as we change ourselves, those around us have to change and their change affects those near them. We can help others change who want to change.

Powerful, yes! Let yourself feel that power. It is within all of us. Let us release that power, that energy, and make good use of it.

If you have picked up this book, you are already in recovery. Just by your willingness to pick up this book, positive energy has led you to be open and to be curious. That is very very powerful.

You have begun a new step, the next step on your journey . . . A very heroic journey.

> *Perhaps some of us have to go through*
> *dark and devious ways before we can find the river of peace,*
> *or the highroad to the soul's destination.*
>
> *Frederick Pierce*

Going Back . . .

My self-consciousness began in the fifth grade, when we moved from Detroit back to Boston, my birthplace and the home of my father's and mother's immediate family. (I lived with my family in Detroit from the time that I was two and a half until I was ten years old.) Until this return to my birthplace, I remember feeling a freedom, living in the world of spontaneity. I was a tomboy and it was just fine. I played ball with the boys, jumped rope and played jacks with the girls. I dug foxholes in the backyard and nearby empty lots, climbed trees and even put on skits for parents with all the kids in the neighborhood, singing and dancing without being self-conscious. I remember these years as being open, comfortable and very alive when I was with people outside my home.

But we returned to Massachusetts as the poor members of the family. My father was out of work. We had to live with rich relatives in their 17-room house where I was constantly reminded to be careful and good. "We're lucky to have a place to stay," my mother told us.

Here, I remember being teased about my poor voice and laughed at when I sang a song I had learned in school.

"You get your bad voice from your mother," my uncle said teasingly.

I felt hot with shame. I was overwhelmed with embarrassment and it was many years before I ever again sang alone in front of even one person!

We moved in with another "rich" aunt in Brookline that summer who teased me "lovingly" about how I had wet her red velvet couch when I was little and how she and my uncle had to reupholster it to get rid of the stain.

"Be very good," my mother warned. "Remember, we have a place to stay only because of the generosity of your aunt."

We moved two more times while I was in the fifth grade until we finally settled in Brookline, a town of well-to-do Jewish families or poor Goyim (non-Jews), as my parents called them.

From then on I learned that I was *never as good as* . . . whomever . . . anyone who was Jewish . . . and that I was *never good enough*.

I very quickly began to close down. I see today that my pain, my shame, my feelings of inadequacy began to enclose me. I felt as if I were less than, living in a much smaller, more restricted world than I had lived in before. It was much smaller than was healthy.

In many respects I stopped growing at this point. My creativity flourished for a while. But even that was stifled by being told that I was alone too much and I should be spending more time with friends.

"What's wrong with you?" I was asked over and over again when I went up to my room to paint or stayed in my room to write.

I was taken to a child psychologist to see what was wrong with Ruth. The family said, "She is now painting in black and she's so thin, you can count every rib on her body."

Part of my soul had begun to dry up and shrivel like a prune. I began to become withdrawn, turning in to myself and my own creativity. This period began many years of hardly ever feeling good with other people unless I had a drink or a drug.

2

STRESS

Complete freedom from stress is death.

Hans Selye, M.D.

Life is full of stress. We all have stress. We can't completely get away from it unless we dull our brains with alcohol and/or drugs or have a lobotomy.

In this last decade there has been a tremendous amount of research that has proven what many have known for centuries. There is an absolute and direct relationship between stress and disease.

But stress can be a positive factor when it pushes us to change and grow: it serves as a warning signal to save our lives. Research is telling us what matters is not how much stress we have in our lives, but how we deal with it. If we feel in control, powerful over a situation, then we can handle our stress and move on. When we have the opportunity to express our stress, we can move on.

Stress does us harm when we feel hopeless and helpless. We are harmed when we suppress our stress. When we are not able to vent our emotions, stress will do us considerable damage.

The Flight Or Fight Response

The real problem today is that our bodies respond to stress as they have always done since the days of cave people. Although society has changed, in some respects our bodies have not. The human body still maintains the warning system which was needed for the very survival of our ancestors many thousands of years ago.

Physiologically we are equipped with much the same system as animals have in order to cope with stress. Our bodies still want to deal with threat as animals do. We want to stay and fight or take flight from frightening situations. But we cannot act on these responses, as did our ancestors, because they are no longer appropriate in our society.

We cannot scream when frustrated if we are in a crowded store. We cannot hit a neighbor when we feel threatened. We cannot jump up and down and hit the walls if we find ourselves stuck in a crowded elevator in a state of panic. Instead we suppress this natural desire to respond by internalizing our distress.

However, our bodies still remain in a state of stress preparedness. Tension remains and we do not relax back to a peaceful, balanced state.

> "Messages are transmitted throughout the neuroendocrine system which causes significant changes in your biochemistry. When an animal is aroused to fight or flight, a similar biochemical reaction quickly takes place. But once the animal has taken action by fighting or fleeing, its neurophysiological stress response subsides and its body rebounds into a state of deep relaxation and ultimately back towards homeostasis. But human beings may have no socially acceptable action to take. Since the negative psychological state persists, the physiological stress response also continues. It is under these circumstances when a stress response is prolonged and unabated that the biochemical changes associated with stress become potentially detrimental to health." (1)

Imagine that you are crossing the street. You have checked both ways and are confident that you are safe. Suddenly, you hear a siren getting louder and louder. Before you can move, a police car has turned the corner and is coming right at you!

In a split second you have triggered the *flight or fight* response automatically. Without even having to think, you race back to the curb. You are safe! Your heart is pounding, your breath is fast, your blood pressure is up, your pupils are dilated and all the natural chemicals in your body are doing their job. As soon as you become aware that you are safe, your body returns to a deep state of relaxation and ultimately back to homeostasis or equilibrium.

Now imagine a time when you found yourself in a stressful situation when you did not feel you had the freedom to express it. Perhaps there was a time when you were scolded by a teacher at school. Perhaps a parent ordered you not to cry. Perhaps you thought you had to act strong and brave in front of a younger child in order to set an example. Maybe a parent came home drunk when you had a friend playing at your house. Whatever the case, imagine all those automatic changes happening in your body. Imagine all those automatic reactions instantly taking place, and you are just standing there, holding yourself back from visibly reacting on the outside.

Gradually the internal reactions stop. But you are left with stress and upset. Your body does not go back to deep relaxation. *You are not in balance.*

When we are unable to find a healthy way to release our stress, we become victims of chronic stress, that is, stress that is held in the body and not released. Dr. Hans Selye, one of the earlier pioneers of stress, discovered that chronic stress suppresses the immune system which is responsible for engulfing cancerous cells. Selye stated that chronic stress produces hormonal imbalance which can lead to high blood pressure, eventual damage to the kidneys and can reinforce chemical imbalance. Hormonal changes over-ride the mechanisms responsible for reducing and adjusting hormonal imbalance which continues the negative and life-threatening cycle.

The *flight or fight response* actually works like this:

A danger arises.

There is a split-second inborn response. Stimulation goes to the hypothalamus and the lower parts of the brain. The hypothalamus signals to the pituitary gland. ACTH hormone is sent to the adrenal glands. Cortical steroids are secreted and flow through the glands. This sets off an outpouring of adrenaline into the circulating blood system.

The blood vessels of the skin contract and blood is forced away from the extremities and into the muscle of the vital organs. The heartbeat increases; blood pressure rises. Simultaneously, adrenaline in the liver chemically converts stored glycogen into active blood sugar (glucose) for fueling nerve and muscle cells with extra energy.

At the same time more adrenaline dilates the bronchi in the lungs to allow a maximum intake of oxygen; dilates the pupils of the eyes (the startle response); contracts the spleen, forcing out its reserve supply of red blood cells; activates chemicals that speed up coagulation of the blood in the event of injury, and increases the tension of voluntary muscles. All this takes place in a split second. Ultimately, when this stress response is prolonged and not released, biochemical changes occur which become detrimental to your health. (2)

What we normally feel when all this is going on is that we begin to breathe fast and shallow, our palms get sweaty and our mouth is dry. Our heart is pounding, our blood pressure is up, our muscles are tense, pupils are dilated and our skin might be covered with goose bumps. (3)

We Learn To Protect Ourselves

Just as the flight or fight instinct is natural and happens automatically, children also automatically protect themselves from the pain, fears and insecurities of early childhood in other ways. They might go numb or repress memories, for instance.

John Bradshaw says that Sigmund Freud was the first to define the primary ego defenses that are automatically used for self-preservation and activated in the face of a threat. (4)

First we go into *denial*, telling ourselves or others that nothing is wrong or what we are told is not true or what we see is not there. Second is *repression*, when our emotions are shamed. Children numb out so they won't feel.

Repressed emotions = numbness = erased experience.

Other automatic defenses include:

Dissociation: Instant numbing after which we go off into a fantasy.

Displacement: When we visualize ourselves somewhere else.

Depersonalization: Seeing ourselves as an object.

Feelings conversion: When one is forbidden to feel shameful or angry so those feelings are converted into acceptable feelings as sadness or guilt.
Somatic conversion: Getting sick when sickness is rewarded in the family.
Projection: When the feelings that are suppressed and denied in ourselves are noticed in someone else.
Inhibitions: Acting out with kindness which stops one's own feelings of shame.
Mental preoccupation: Which can distract one from one's own feelings; turning away from oneself.
Rationalization, minimization, explanation, sublimation and *compensation.*

As Bradshaw says, these defenses were the best decisions available at the time. They kept you sane. They literally saved your life. But the very defenses that were once life-giving, later on became the very preservers of our toxic shame. (5)

Alice Miller writes in the *Drama of the Gifted Child* that in these instances the true self had been in a state of noncommunication because it had to be protected. (6)

Later, as adults, these people will only admit those feelings that are accepted and approved by their inner censor. Depression and a sense of inner emptiness is the price they must pay for this control. The true self cannot communicate because it has remained unconscious and undeveloped in its inner prison. (7)

Chronic Stress/Shock

Wayne Kritsberg says that during the state of shock, certain events happen to both the emotional and physical aspects of the person experiencing the shock. (8)

On the physical level, the body gears itself up to manage the disaster. Some of the physical changes that occur:

Breath patterns change.
Adrenaline is released into the system.
Heart rate quickens and the blood pressure elevates.
Eyes may appear vacant and distant.
Face may lose color and appear greyish.
Skin may feel cold to touch.
Emotionally the person shuts down and becomes numb.

Shock and recovery from the shock state usually conform to the following model:

1. Reaction to the catastrophe.
2. Rebound stage — feelings begin to be felt.
3. Resolution stage — resolving the feelings of fear, anger, loss, etc., experienced as a result of the original trauma.

Catastrophe/Trauma = Shock State = Rebound = Resolution

Shutting down is normal in the shock state. If one does not have a chance to process one's feelings, a piece of your emotional life will be repressed and stay that way. All through your life a part of you will stay in shock. This is *chronic shock.*

> *Chronic shock* is the experiencing of the catastrophic event, and not resolving the physical/psychological effects of the catastrophe. Many adult children from alcoholic families, because of the inherent nature of the alcoholic family, suffer from chronic shock . . . (9)

In a healthy family a child has an opportunity to process feelings and get emotional resolution through love and support.

While Kritberg talks about the alcoholic family, all families who are other-addicted, co-dependent or dysfunctional respond in the same way. Any shocking event, such as divorce, sexual abuse, or the death of a parent, puts children under great stress. If they cannot express their grief, they will stay in this state of shock. If asked how they were feeling the children would probably say "Fine," meaning that they were not feeling anything.

> Silence engulfs the family. No one talks about the incident. The child is left to interpret what the trauma means, which often takes the form of the child blaming himself for the occurrence of the traumatic event. Because of the alcoholic family rule of *"No Talk,"* the child has no one to turn to and the feelings stay bottled up inside, shutting down emotionally. A part of the child becomes numb and stays that way. Memory loss often occurs and the child loses the ability to recall the event. The child may also dissociate from the event, and although he may be able to recall the trauma, it might be remembered as if it happened to another person. When the shock is not resolved, the *chronic shock state occurs* which will remain until it is treated and resolved. (10)

Some characteristics of people suffering from *chronic shock*:

A narrow range of emotional experiences.
A feeling of going numb when faced with a difficult situation.

Poor or no memory recall around traumatic events.
Shortened attention span.
Confused thinking caused by overwhelming fear experienced at the time of the trauma.
A feeling of hopelessness and helplessness.
A lack of being able to feel joy and happiness.
Intense feelings at inappropriate times.
Denial that the event had any effect.

> *When we are not allowed to remember, to express our feelings and to grieve or mourn our losses or traumas, whether real or threatened, through the free expression of our Child Within, we become ill.*
>
> *Charles Whitfield (11)*

Going Back . . .

Debbie was 12 years old the day that her father and I told our three children that we were getting a divorce. She is now 29 and cannot remember any of these details. Debbie and her brother and sister, who were ten and eight respectively, were called into the kitchen for a family talk. I still remember this scene 17 years later as if it were today. Her father and I explained that I needed some time to get my life straightened out. I planned to go away for a while. After drinking almost daily for the last 17 years of my life, I was finally in recovery and had been sober for six months. I needed some time by myself to sort out my life.

Debbie tore out of the room crying and gagging and ran into the bathroom. Her father demanded in a deep and threatening voice: "You come back here! You get into this room right now!"

She did come back, tears streaming down her face, body stiff, arms tight along her body, fists clenched. I reached out to her but she remained stiff and tensed.

Later on, I sought to have joint custody. I fought a hard, messy and bitter legal fight but lost after six and a half hours in court. Since that time I have done everything I can to maintain a close relationship with my children, always letting them know how much I love them and that the divorce had nothing to do with them. Together we have continued to work through this painful change and have, gratefully, loving and healthy relationships today.

For many years I regretted that I did not tell my husband to let Debbie alone that day, to let her stay by herself in the bathroom and have her own experience of her feelings. I regretted for years that I did not have the courage to speak up, insist that he leave Debbie alone and let her have her feelings. But I was too full of my own fears and guilt at what harm I might be causing my children by not having them live with me. I did not have the confidence to say what I thought was right at that time.

My daughter has no memory of that shock-filled day and little memory of much prior to then because she has blocked out much of the first 12 years of her life. She closed down when she was not allowed to feel her feelings. And in the years that followed she did not receive therapy to help her through this time.

Because I did not get joint custody of my children, I had no legal rights in their lives. My opinion that therapy was critical for all the children was ignored. My daughter stayed closed and angry for many years. It was not until a marriage of her own ended painfully that she began to seek treatment and begin her own recovery, her own healing process.

Life insists, in each form it takes, that the line must be drawn at one's endurance. One must say to protect all that pervades the inner chambers, here is the line. This is the limit: I cannot step beyond.

Samantha Mooney (12)
"A Snowflake In My Hand"

Post-Traumatic Stress Disorder

Some Vietnam veterans have been identified as experiencing Post Traumatic Stress Disorder (PTSD). Lloyd F. Humphrey, in an article he wrote in 1988, has described many similarities that Kritsberg has described as *chronic shock.* The disruption of the normal "Grief Cycle," which is necessary for adjusting to significant loss, has not happened in the dysfunctional home or for the Vietnam vet. Therefore, until this can happen in a safe and healthy place, the person continues to suffer and stay stuck.

Humphrey says that the normal cycle of loss, anger, denial, depression, guilt, acceptance and reconstruction was interrupted in many Vietnam vet somewhere between the anger and denial stages. Not having the time or support to take care of themselves during combat, the vets had used alcohol and drugs to mask their symptoms so they could go on with their missions.

> While grief will occur to individuals engaged in normal activities during a lifetime, a lifetime of grief can be compressed into a few days, even a few hours of combat. This grief was buried and not allowed to surface or be dealt with for years. (13)

While men who went to Vietnam had performed their duty, just as soldiers in other wars, they came home to people who had turned against them. They learned not to talk about their experiences, just as children in dysfunctional families learn not to talk about what goes on at home.

The returning vets would try to go on with their lives, not understanding why they would cry, or feel like crying, and fly into terrible and destructive rages for no apparent reason. These reactions often led to alcohol and drugs as a way of life. For many, the only time that sleep was possible was after getting drunk or stoned.

Gradually, over a period of years, repetitious symptoms have been identified — symptoms recognized as being the same as those experienced by survivors of natural disasters, such as earthquakes and tidal waves when great losses of human life and property occur. But the Vietnam vets had more subtle symptoms which were caused by long-term masking of the grief process, was now stuck somewhere between anger and denial.

> Over a period of time the original trauma of the combat, masked by chemical use, had been buried under layers of subsequent traumas that occur to heavy alcohol or drug users — loss of spouse and children, jobs and friends. The vet was now suffering from PTSD or *Delayed Stress*. This has been compared to knowing you are stepping on a "Bouncing Betty," a land mine that is activated when you step on it, and explodes when you step off it. (13)

Humphrey writes that symptoms of PTSD-Chronic and/or Delayed Stress are . . .

1. *Depression:* Many Vietnam vets are chronically depressed, have feelings of worthlessness, sleep disturbances, difficulties concentrating and will cry if they recall experiences in Vietnam.
2. *Isolation:* Many vets live alone or profess they would like to. They feel distant from nonveteran peers like "old men in young bodies." They have few friends and have frequently gone through multiple marriages.
3. *Rage:* Vietnam veterans at times feel rage that is so intense, it causes them to strike out at anything and everyone, including loved ones.
4. *Avoidance of feelings and alienation:* The veterans often describe themselves as being "emotionally dead" and are thought of as cold blooded by family and friends. This stems from the Vietnam experience, where people were dehumanized. The natives were described as "Gooks," "Slopes" or "Dinks." Your buddy was "zapped," not killed. The enemy was "wasted," not shot to death.
5. *Survival Guilt:* Many veterans feel that they survived at the expense of another's life.
6. *Anxiety Reactions:* Many veterans are hypervigilant, will not cross an open area and over-react to loud noises. Many possess weapons and will even sleep with a loaded gun. They sit in rooms, back to the wall, their eyes constantly moving to take in the areas around them.
7. *Sleep Disturbances and Nightmares:* The veteran suffering from PTSD often is unable to sleep unless totally exhausted. Many cannot sleep unless self-medicated with alcohol and/or drugs.
8. *Intrusive Thoughts:* These are often compared to daydreams, when the veteran has a "flashback" of combat scenes. These can be triggered by sounds, odors or scenes re-

mindful of Vietnam, e.q., the slapping sound of helicopter blades, cars backfiring or the odor of a burning substance.

Humphrey goes on to say that to treat vets for alcoholism and drug abuse is not enough. They will continue to use alcohol and/ or drugs to block out memories if they are not treated for the underlying disorder symptoms generated by Vietnam combat.

3

INTRODUCING ENDORPHINS

The brain doesn't care
whether psychological pain is caused by a
distant father or a misfiring endorphin;
its response will be the same.

Turkington

Robert Ornstein and David Sobel in their book *The Healing Brain* write that it now appears there may be hundreds of different chemical messenger molecules and that these neurotransmitters are the "words" which the brain uses to communicate. They describe the brain at work as being like millions of miniature explosions going on and off each instant as neurons fire their electrical charges. Inside these neurons are scores of chemicals being released, going from cell to cell and back. (1)

The key to understanding how the brain communicates through this array of chemical messages lies in the shape of the chemicals and their receptors. Distributed throughout the body on the surfaces of cell membranes are hundreds, perhaps thousands, of different

> types of molecular structures called receptors. Each type of receptor has a characteristic three-dimensional shape and, like a lock, can only be opened or activated by a chemical key with the correct corresponding shape. (1)

They also found that with certain types of stress the brain appears to trigger certain types of endorphins along with ACTH from the pituitary gland. The ACTH is a signal to the adrenal glands to prepare for fight or flight, while the endorphins may help block pain so that the organism can take action without being completely distracted. (2)

Many researchers regard adrenaline as the "fear hormone" and noradrenaline as the "anger hormone." (3)

Endorphins are neurotransmitters in our brain that act like opium. They may alleviate pain, produce euphoria under some circumstances or act as a sedative. They are secreted by certain nerve cells of the brain and can produce feelings of well-being or relief from pain.

Curiosity has led me to many books which describe these chemical and hormonal functions. I am a recovering alcoholic, sober for over 17 years, a founder and former director for 14 years of a treatment program for chemically dependent women and their families, and an author of three books about recovery.* The reason that I am going into such depth here to explain this connection of mind/body, stress and the chemistry of our brain is so that those of you who might not have any idea how this all works can follow with me on the next steps.

Years ago, after finishing my first book *The Journey Within: A Spiritual Path To Recovery,* I began reading and thinking about endorphins, the hormone that gives us our sense of well-being and is our body's natural pain killer. I went to the library, trying to track down as much information as I could and began asking questions.

My early thoughts led me to ask the following:

- Endorphins are our body's natural pain killer. They give us a sense of well being. Is it possible that the bodies of those of us who have grown up in alcoholic or dysfunctional

---

***The Journey Within: A Spiritual Path To Recovery, Learning To Live In The Now* and *Time For Joy,* all published by Health Communications, Inc.

homes, with all their stress and pain, have closed down their ability to produce endorphins?
- And doesn't it naturally follow that if we no longer have the ability to feel good, as other "normal" people do, we may chase this good feeling in many directions in our lives?

Many of us chased it into alcohol, drugs and other addictions.

My research at first yielded very little about endorphins, but the amount of information has gradually increased with each year. During this time a new science has developed called *psychoneuroimmunology.* Through it we have learned more and more about the connection between the brain, the nervous system and our bodies. Science now has proof that we are what we think we are. Our bodies respond to our thoughts and our thoughts respond to our bodies. It has also been proven that stress affects all aspects of our health, including our immune systems.

And as we began hearing more and more about the devastating killer disease AIDS, my curiosity took me one step further with the following questions:

- Is it possible that a large number of the people who have AIDS have grown up in alcoholic, drug dependent or dysfunctional homes?
- Since they have a depletion of endorphins and do not deal well with stress, do they have a weaker immune system and are therefore more susceptible to diseases?

I first began recording these theories on July 6, 1986. I questioned many people about the subject for a few years but no one knew of such a link. Since then I have read about many connections. By the time this book is published, much of what I originally thought of as theory will be backed up by facts.

Let's find out more about endorphins and why this knowledge is so potentially powerful to our well-being.

Getting Better Acquainted With Endorphins

When I guide people to work with the idea of endorphins, I like to picture them as little smiling red hearts, floating eagerly in a storage box in the back of our heads, just waiting to be released.

If the next few pages seem too technical for you, please don't be concerned. Simply pick up the basic ideas. It is not something you have to remember to understand the rest of this book. It is here for those who want a larger, more detailed picture. Please believe me when I say that you can make positive changes in your life without having this knowledge.

Dr. Bernie Siegal in *Peace, Love And Healing* describes our cells in what I found to be a very simple way. He writes that each cell in our brain has a *tentacle* and a *dendrite.* The dendrite communicates with the tentacle of another cell through connections called *synapses.* They communicate with one another through chemicals in the brain called *neurotransmitters.* There is a gap or space between each cell so their communication happens through these chemicals. There are billions of nerve cells giving off different signals at different times. (4)

Dr. Siegal goes on to explain that the *peptide* messenger molecules manufactured by the brain and the immune system are the link. There are approximately 60 known peptide molecules in the body including endorphins. (5) There are many more expected to be found.

Endorphins are opium-like neurotransmitters in our brain. They may alleviate pain, produce euphoria under some circumstances or act as a sedative. They are secreted at the tip of the connection of the brain cell.

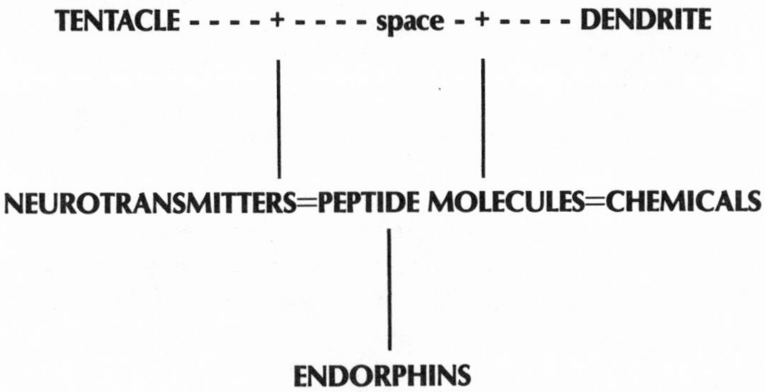

For example, many of us know the feeling produced by endorphins as "runner's high," which is followed by a sense of well-being. Under some circumstances, however, endorphins may act as a sedative.

Dr. Herbert Benson in *Your Maximum Mind* describes the basic building block of the brain as being a single cell or a neuron. He suggests cells may be pictured as living factories, which utilize blood-transported oxygen and sugar as fuel. This fuel, through well-defined biochemical steps, produces the energy that makes possible a vast number of biological tasks required to maintain the life of the cell. Cells interact with other cells to produce thoughts and actions. If the brain cell is deprived of its fuel, which comes primarily from the food we eat and the air we breathe, it will die.

The latest research shows that our bodies and minds are different expressions of the same information—and that information is carried by the peptide.

> In humans, animals, plants, eggs, seeds and on down to one-celled organisms, the peptides are the messenger molecules that carry the information from state to state. In man they make possible the move from perception or thought or feeling in the mind, to messages transmitted to the brain, to hormonal secretions and down to cellular action in the body — then back again to the mind

> and brain, in a never-ending feedback loop. The key juncture in the loop, the place where body and mind meet and cross over through the action of the peptides, is in the limbic/hypothalamic area of the brain. It is here that scientists have found dense numbers of receptors clustered together in what they call "hotspots." Peptides fit into these receptors, key and lock fashion, to activate the inner workings of the cells on which the receptors are located. (6)
>
> Herbert Benson

Kindling

Dr. Benson suggests that parts of the brain are the sites of anxiety-provoked reactions. These areas may become extremely sensitive and more susceptible to arousal by repeated exposure to internal and external pressures.

This neurological hypersensitivity may involve a process known as *kindling* in the brain tissues. *Kindling* refers to the phenomenon of repeated stimulation of certain parts of the brain that results in a sensitizing of those parts. As a result they respond easily to a little less stimulation and more powerfully to average stimulation.

Benson states that repeated exposure to stresses and pressures activate the arousal mechanisms of the brain and make arousal more likely in ways that are physically and emotionally debilitating. For instance, some individuals whose brains have been kindled or sensitized may be inclined to experience serious anxiety or panic attacks more repeatedly than others who are less sensitized. As situations become worse and worse, new neural pathways or wiring develops. The individual develops the habit of responding excessively to all stress, whether it is extreme or minor.

What is important here is that just as the brain can change in negative ways from stress, it can also return to a more positive set of pathways. (7)

Endorphins are also present in our pituitary and intestinal tracts as well as in our brains. Our bodies use endorphins to relieve psychological as well as physical pain. If good touching and talking produce natural feelings of well-being, both emotionally and physically, what happens to our body's ability to produce endorphins when we are in a great deal of stress? What happens to us when we do not feel good physically or emotionally? When we do not feel worthwhile or have a positive sense of self worth?

If we have a genetically weak endorphin system, we may get inadequate release of the neuropeptides and be particularly sensitive to psychological pain. Similarly if we have a strong endorphin system but constantly perceive situations as stressful and threatening, we may also experience frequent distress and possible depression from *depleting our endorphin supply.* (8)

Pain

When we are in pain it ordinarily signals prompt recuperation by motivating our bodies to withdraw, recuperate and heal. Ornstein and Sobel explain that sometimes in pain we have to act quickly to save ourselves. In certain times of stress, for example if you were to touch a hot stove, the brain appears to trigger the release of certain kinds of endorphins along with ACTH from the pituitary gland. This is a signal to the adrenal glands to prepare for fight or flight, while the endorphins may help block pain so that the body may take action without being completely distracted. Stress and pain are important clues for turning on the pain relief system and releasing endorphins. (9)

Placebos And Faith

Placebos are sugar pills with no medicinal value. Many tests have been made that have proven the power of the mind over the body and the connection of mind-body. Placebos have been experimented with for years to *increase* the understanding of the mind-body connection.

In thousands of tests, patients have been divided into two groups. One group will get a real medication, the other half a placebo. They will all be told what effect to expect. In many tests even the doctors and nurses do not know who is getting what. The net results often show that a large number of patients in *both* groups experience the results they were told to expect. Bernie Siegal says that the key word here is *expect*. What we expect often does happen. It has been proven over and over again that if you have a belief that you will get well, your chances of getting well are much stronger.

> It is the expectations aroused by the substance or procedure that are ultimately responsible for the result. (10)

About one third of the people treated with placebos report positive results. (11)

Dr. Martin L. Rossman in his book *The Healing Power of Imagery* writes that the important thing about the placebo response is that it demonstrates beyond doubt that thoughts can trigger the body's own self-healing abilities.

The patients imagine that the pills they are ingesting are effective. This positive image triggers positive thoughts which trigger the healing chemicals to be released. Rossman calls imagery the interface language between body and mind and it can allow illness to become a teacher of wellness. (12)

One study done in 1981 with students at the University of Tennessee Center for Health Sciences proved that thoughts alone can increase the endorphin levels of the body. They measured the endorphin levels of 32 patients suffering from chronic pain. The doctors gave all the patients placebos. Fourteen, over 40%, of the patients felt better! Positive thoughts raised endorphin levels and in turn the endorphins blocked the pain. (13)

Other peptide rich areas are the linings of the gut and stomach, which can be turned on for pain relief by using placebos if people strongly believe they will work.

Psychoneuroimmunology, or PSI, is a new scientific discipline in which neuroscientists, psychologists and immunologists work together to explore the body's most subtle interconnections.

Joan Borysenko, Ph.D., in her book *Minding The Body, Mending The Mind,* tells us that much PSI research centers on the neuropeptide messengers, secreted by the brain, into the immune system and by the nerve cells into various other organs. What scientists have found is that areas of the brain that control emotion are particularly rich receptors for these chemicals. At the same time the brain also has receptor sites for molecules produced by the immune system alone — the lymphokines and interleukins. What we see, then, is a rich and intricate two-way communication system linking the mind, the immune system and potentially all other systems, a pathway through which our emotions — our hopes and fears — can affect the body's ability to defend itself. (14)

Candace Pert, called the Mother of Endorphins, is a neuropharmacologist of the National Institute of Mental Health. She has predicted that the chemicals we produce in our own brains will become the basis of many therapies of the future. She is already using Peptide T (the laboratory produced clone of one of these natural chemicals) in AIDS patients with striking results. (15)

She makes an extraordinary statement:

> We know that the same neuropeptides secreted by the brain can also facilitate the movement of white blood cells of the immune system to a locus of injury. So why could you not direct it consciously? . . . It's a wild idea in that there is no experimental proof for it — yet there is nothing that excludes the possibility either. (16)

Other Important Chemicals

Serotonin (sir-o-tone-in)

Serotonin is a transmitter that helps regulate our moods and like endorphins, it seems to relieve pain. An increase in serotonin apparently raises the activity of endorphins and enkephalins. A person who has a genetically weak endorphin system may have supersensitivity to psychological pain and under stress be particularly vulnerable to depression. As with other disorders, both genetic and environmental factors often act on the brain and produce depression. Serotonin is an inhibitor of activity and behavior and is also important in the sleep-wake cycle. (17)

It has been found that depressed people coming from alcoholic families have lower levels of serotonin metabolite than was the case with depressives having no family history of alcoholism. Blair Justice suggests that a person with a low serotonin system and a coping style of being negative about everything may be at the highest risk. (18)

Other research has shown that low levels of serotonin have been found both in people who commit suicide and in people who are alcoholic. (19)

Norepinephrine (nor' ep-in-ef-rine)

Norepinephrine is also a neurotransmitter but it has the opposite effect of serotonin. It produces an alerting, attention focusing, orienting response, sensory arousal and motor and autonomic priming for "fight or flight." (20)

Norepinephrine seems to be necessary for focusing properly on stimuli and environment. In depression, with the disturbance in the norepinephrine system, a person does not receive or process information without distortion.

Some depressed people have a defect in brain regulation of adrenal secretion, particularly corticosteroids, leaving them vulnerable to excess stress hormones.

Our thinking styles and learning experiences change cell structures within the nervous system. (21)

A chronic stress reaction can result when an imbalance of neurochemicals are released by the hypothalamus. This is triggered by unregulated transmitters in other parts of the brain. It can lead to an imbalance of pituitary hormones and an excess of cortisol from the adrenal cortex.

Western people are children of inner poverty,
though outwardly we have everything. Probably no other
people in history have been so lonely, so alienated,
so confused over values, so neurotic.

Robert Johnson

Jennifer, a client of mine, shared the following story of her childhood:

It was close to 7 PM. The doorbell would ring at any moment. I felt my body become even more tense. My hands were clenched and damp and my breath was short and shallow. This was a nightly ritual. As soon as we heard the doorbell ring, my brother and I would race to the bathroom. Whoever got there first would slam the door shut and lock themselves in, safe for that evening. The loser would then be left to open the door and stand at the top of the stairs, waiting while the slow, staggering footsteps became louder and louder, wait while the heavy feet climbed the three flights to the top apartment, the sounds finally taking on the shape of a man who was our father. The loser had to stand there and kiss him hello because that is what he insisted upon. That is what his father had demanded of him. That is what he demanded of us: respect. He demanded respect.

If we were not there, he would yell for us, saying that he was home and we should be there to greet him. His breath would reek of scotch and his face would become red from his shouting. There was often yelling and shouting . . . the threat of a beating hung in the air. Sometimes he would whip off his belt and swing it threateningly. We were rarely actually hit. Just the threat . . . it was always there, depending on what his mood was when he came home. Depending on how much he had to drink. Depending on how his day had gone and how well he could handle how much he had drunk.

If his day had not gone well, he might be full of anger and vent that on my mother and us. Or he might be full of self-pity, and his drinking would precipitate heavy sobs and tears. There actually were days that went well. After drinks with friends or the boss, he might come home jovial and expansive and he even surprise us with a gift or promise of a future treat. We never knew which mood he would be in so we had to be prepared in the only way that we knew how . . . by running to the bathroom. He would accept that as a legitimate excuse for not giving him full respect, whether he deserved it or not.

There was a period of our growing up when this was a nightly event. It occurred when my father's drinking had accelerated. Life had not gone the way that he hoped it would. He had experienced business failures and had to start over again many times. As he grew older, each time was harder to begin again.

This last time he was determined to make his job work, maybe because he thought he might not have another chance. He would get up at 4 o'clock in the morning to be at work by 5:30 A.M. He worked hard and within just a few years had worked his way up from a 50-year-old stock boy to foreman in the shipping department with over 200 men working under him.

By now he was full of old anger and resentments and he was tired. As the years went on, he could handle his drinking less and less and took his moods out more and more on us. He resented his long hours at work. He resented that he was now working indoors. He loved the out-of-doors and had been happy when he was a traveling salesperson.

What is the physical, emotional and spiritual damage to children growing up with such tension? Jennifer's story is mild compared to many others. She was not physically abused, although the threat was often there. Hundreds of thousands of children are physically abused. And many thousands more are sexually abused. We hear about them everyday now. Some of their stories make the news. These stories used to be secrets. Their secrets used to be locked up in the closets of their minds. Many still die because of their secrets. Their pain is too great. Thank God we are beginning to talk. We are just beginning to dare to share our pain.

Many are just beginning to dare and then to trust that God or a parent, an uncle, a brother or teacher will not strike them dead if they tell the truth.

Jennifer told me:

When I was very little, my father was a different person. He shared his joy of life and the out-of-doors with me as he took me pony riding and taught me how to fly a kite and ride a bike. He took me skiing, swimming and fishing, and shared with me the joys of a sunset and the peace of a quiet lake. Those memories would return years later and I was able to feel love for this man, my father. But not until years later, not until I had experienced my own many years of drinking. Not until I had finally gone into recovery for myself because of my own alcoholism. And not until, even much later, when I had gone into recovery as an adult child of an alcoholic.

How Does All This Relate To Those Who Have Grown Up In An Alcoholic Or Dysfunctional Home?

Remember that stress is normal. In a home that is healthy and supportive, where parents not only allow, but encourage full expression of feelings, we experience . . .

Stress which creates *tension.*

We *vent* tension by expressing our feelings.

The *danger passes.*

We *relax.*

How we feel today has a great deal to do with what our lives were like in our earlier years and the love and support we either received or didn't. Those of us who have not been encouraged and given the freedom to express and release our tension, are left with our stress.

It is common for a person to go into one stressful situation after another without any relief. It is common to be in a constant state of tension. Imagine a child who is always wondering what kind of mood the alcoholic parent will be in, whether they will be drunk when they come up the stairs or whether the child will be the brunt of a bad mood. That child is always alert, never relaxed, just waiting for the next reprimand, the next beating, the next embarrassment or the next threat.

These are the children who grow up with what is now called *The Laundry List,* typical rules of an alcoholic or dysfunctional family that keep its members in a state of disease where children are told . . . (22)

- Not to talk about what is going on to anyone outside the house.
- Not to show feelings.

- Not to cry.
- Not to act out.
- Not to be angry.

They are taught to ignore stress, to deny it, or to suppress it.

In short, children are told *not to be who they are* with messages such as: "Be quiet. Your father had a hard day." And "How could you think that? After all we've done for you."

These messages are mild compared to the destructive imprints that are left with sexual and physical abuse. Threats for one's life, such as, "If you tell anyone, I'll kill you!" have been among the reasons that many have carried the secrets of sexual abuse with them for years. For some this secret lasted their entire lives until alcohol, drugs or suicide put an end to their pain. Others dared to tell and were told that it was their fault and would not have happened if they had not provoked or allowed it to happen. Ultimately their secrets became buried under layers and layers of guilt, shame and low self-esteem.

Messages such as, "If you don't stop crying, I'll really give you something to cry about!" had children huddling in a corner holding their breath so they wouldn't utter a sound.

The damage occurred when they didn't express their stress, not because they experienced it. It's how they reacted to it. The fear of the results they could expect if they expressed their stress caused greater damage than the stressful experience.

Hans Selye, known as the Father of Stress, tells us that it is not the stress that counts in these instances, but how we handle it.

The children were usually left with feeling wrong, unworthy, and in a constant state of fear, always alert to what would be next. So they tightened up and never relaxed. They never had a sense of self-worth or well-being. There was always a hunger, always a wanting, a reaching out to bring in, to fill that empty space inside, a knowing that something was missing, and something was different about them. They were always striving to feel all right.

Thus they stuffed their feelings until they didn't know they had any. Finally they could no longer feel joy or love because they were too full of frozen pain, fear and rage.

All our memories are stored in our brains as in a computer. Our brains store the memory of all our experiences. The memory is actually our perception of our experience, not the experience itself. Because of our early traumatic memories, fear and anxiety set up reactions that in later life continue to act in the same way as when we were threatened even though no threat actually still exists. When a new experience comes up for us, our body responds as if the old experiences were happening again.

Old experiences *can be* wiped out so that we can learn to live in the now with only what is actually happening at the moment and we can learn to be free, and positive.

Kenneth Pellietier writes that stress disorders are based upon the slow developmental accumulation of psychological and physical stress responses throughout the life of the individual. (23) He adds that normal adaptive stress reaction occurs when the stress is definable.

For example, you are in college and exams are approaching. Stress builds in your body and you are full of fear and discomfort. You are even more susceptible to sickness at this time because stress weakens the immune system. When exams are over, your body returns to its normal state. The exams are a clear and identifiable source of stress.

> "However, when the source of stress is ambiguous, undefinable or prolonged, or when several sources exist simultaneously, the individual does not return to a normal mental and physiological baseline as rapidly. He or she continues to manifest a potentially damaging stress reaction. This concept is fundamental to understanding psychosomatic disorders." (24)

Without our learning stress management techniques to reduce our responses to inordinate stress, prolonged severe stress can actually alter the cortisol receptors in the hypothalamus. This eliminates the feedback circuit that ordinarily would turn off the stress response. *The reaction to stress would continue even in its absence, eventually producing the diseases of stress.* (25)

Remember, too, that depressed people coming from alcoholic families have been found to have lower levels of serotonin. With a low serotonin system and negative coping, a person is at high risk for sickness.

It is now clear that we can deplete our endorphin supply and be particularly sensitive to psychological pain if we have a genetically weak endorphin system. In this case we may get an inadequate release of the neuropeptides. We can also deplete our endorphin supply even if we have a strong endorphin system but constantly *perceive* situations as stressful and threatening.

We do not have to let the past control our future. We do not have to be victims of dysfunction and abuse or genetic predisposition. It has become clearly obvious that we can do something about how we feel physically, mentally and spiritually. In short, we *can be* in charge of our lives.

4

Finding Relief

When pain creates an emotional need,
the addict turns to the addiction for relief,
just as someone else may turn to a spouse,
a best friend or spiritual beliefs for relief.

Craig Nakken

As we have already seen, prolonged stress shuts down our ability to feel good and to deal with pain and stress. We live with a great longing to feel good and to feel what we perceive others feel. We begin to discover things outside of ourselves to give us that feeling.

Some found healthy ways to relieve stress through sports, creativity or spirituality. Some joined groups, acted in plays, painted, wrote, became political.

Unfortunately, many found relief in alcohol and drugs . . . or

People

We discover that being with people who nurture us and take care of us makes us feel good. People who praise us and need us make us feel good. People who fill the void, the empty space, make us feel good. We eventually come to the point where we think we need these people to feel good about ourselves. When they leave, we find other people. We do not know there might be another way to look for these good feelings in our existing relationships. We want them so much that our constant demands end up pushing them away.

Food

Many found relief in food. Food elements work by supplying the brain cells with what they need for synthesizing certain key neurotransmitters. (1) If the serotonin level has been depleted, eating chocolates will stimulate the flow of serotonin and produce a sense of well-being. How can someone possibly give up chocolates when they have been hurting for so long? When their lives have been full of such pain? Some people get a sense of well-being from pasta and other carbohydrates. Others just by filling up and eating and eating until the pain or the emptiness goes away, or until the suffering from the eating itself replaces the original pain.

Kay Sheppard believes that food addicts have a biological defect handed down from generation to generation. The food addicts seek food to alter their reality. She believes that they have a biogenetic disease and that the answer to this compulsive path to self-destruction lies within the brain itself. (2)

It is interesting to note that all addictive substances start as something natural. For example, heroin is nothing but a plant, a flower. The juice of the poppy is refined into opium, then into morphine and finally into heroin. Sugar is nothing but a chemical taken from the juice of the cane or beet, then refined into molasses, into brown sugar and finally into white crystals. (3)

Sheppard states further that addiction has a biological basis related to the way that the brain uses its neurotransmitters. These transmitters affect a change of balance within the brain which brings about an improved feeling.

The hypothalamus, known as the old brain, is the part of the brain associated with addiction and instinctive feelings. This is the same part of the brain that has our instinctive feelings for survival and governs our functions of flight and fight, production, thirst and hunger. Our primitive instinctive feelings of fear, hunger, anger, thirst and sex drive, the foundations for our basic existence, are found here.

The hypothalamus sends a message to the cortex, the new brain, with a specific request. The cortex decides what to do. Therefore if we are hungry or thirsty, our hypothalamus tells our cortex, which gives us the message to eat or drink.

Sheppard believes that the addict has an aberration of the system, a short circuit in the neurotransmitter service. When an addict needs anything, only the drug of choice will satisfy and restore balance within the survival brain.

The hypothalamus is affected by drugs, food, sex and exercise. When the brain gets the signal that a need exists, the brain responds by releasing chemical signals which cause an action to fill the needs.

Sheppard also propounds the theory that in addiction there is an abnormality of endorphin-enkelephalin metabolism. Whenever a substance or behavior changes the neurotransmitters, producing abnormal metabolism of the neurotransmitter system within the old brain, the result is addiction.

She states that it is possible that the production of enkelephalins and endorphins is low because of either decreased production or rapid destruction in addicted individuals.

When the endorphins are low, the brain is on edge, making addicted individuals susceptible to substances which will artificially soothe the brain and improve feelings. Such substances will bring the brain into balance.

How many times have you said, "I am going to give up this or that" and seen yourself reach for the very thing that you are trying to stay away from?

"Addiction is one of the most stress-producing illnesses of all, and people can only take so much stress before their lives and personalities start to break down. There is a point where a person emotionally, mentally, spiritually and finally physically breaks down under the stress and pain produced by the addiction." (4)

Shutting Down, Withdrawing

Others found relief in turning off, closing down, watching television, living through books and fantasy.

Sex, Thrills, Danger And Excitement

"Adrenaline Rush" is when the adrenal medulla releases stress hormones and causes the entire body to respond with a jolt and a tremendous surge of energy. (5)

Some found relief in thrill-seeking. Some chase thrills in danger, such as mountain-climbing, sky-diving and auto-racing. Some find relief in the excitement of watching the thrill seekers. Some find relief in sex. There is nothing wrong with any of these activities. It is necessary to examine the reasons for doing them, the need to do them and the extent to which they control our lives.

If we feel excited when going to the race track, or making a bet or going shopping, the excitement comes from the flow of hormones. We feel alive and good; we will want more.

Watch a crowd at a football or baseball game, hockey or soccer match. Watch the crowd at the race track. The stimulation! The roar! The screams for more, more, more! Whether it is for the home team or the underdog to win, or the heavy bet to pay off, the endorphins are flowing all over the place during the action. When the action is over, we are either elated or depressed, depending on the side we are on.

People who need this kind of stimulation to feel good will not only be attending sports matches often, but will be glued to games on television or radio and reading the sports pages in the newspapers as soon as they come out. Enormous amounts of money are spent catering to these needs for more and more outside stimulation.

I'll never forget the wonderful, peaceful feeling flowing through me when I drank. I was filled with warmth and softness. I felt a glow. I felt all was finally well with my world.

Going Back . . .

Theory "As Good As . . ."

Scotch. Good scotch. Dewars or J & B. Or Chevas Regal or Haig and Haig Pinch, when someone else was buying or on the rare occasion that I could afford it. I can almost taste it again now, although it has been over 14 years. I loved good scotch. I always thought that I drank because I loved it. I loved swirling it around in a glass full of ice. Actually, three ice cubes were perfect because they would melt just slowly enough to give the scotch a chill, but not so fast that it would be watered down by the time it was finished. The scotch never stayed too long in that glass! I loved the taste of good scotch. I loved the way it felt as it burned in my chest when it went down, and I loved the way that it made me feel. It made me F E E E L good for many years.

Until I could no longer handle it. Until my body became so addicted that it screamed for more and more and I became all about trying not to drink, and then drinking out of control. I remember that when it still made me feel good, I could smile, I could laugh, I could even dance and sing and be "one of" the group and F E E E L good.

Now, years later, I believe that I needed it on levels which I was not even aware of at the time. I now believe that addicts of all kinds need the drug of choice not to get "high" but to get "level," not to escape but to be here like everyone else. They need it to become "average," to *feel as good as* everyone else feels who does not need to stimulate chemicals in their brain to have a sense of well-being. Now I know that I drank to "feel as good as . . ." and just to *feel good. I never* felt as good as others. I *never* felt comfortable in social settings. I *never* felt comfortable in school. I was always uptight, tense and on guard. The only times as a child that I did feel comfortable, even happy, were when I was playing out-of-doors, at school or at camp doing exactly what I loved: playing sports, being outside or by myself, painting or writing.

I remember a period when we lived down the street from Brookline High. One side of the school was a huge wall with no windows at all. I would go there every evening and hit my tennis ball against this wall. Night after night I would compete with myself, trying to see how many times in a row I could hit the ball without missing. I remember having scores up to 700 or 800. My little brother would come out with me on occasion and compete.

As I am writing this and thinking about it for the first time in many years, I can again recapture the *good feelings* I had as I chased that ball. I can hear the sound as it hits my racket and I can feel my breath full and hard. I know today I was stimulating my endorphins. I was *feeling* so good because my body's natural chemical system was working in a healthy way.

5

ADDICTIONS AND COMPULSIONS

The very demand for the repetition of pleasure brings about pain.

Krishnamurti

The gene for alcoholism has now been identified, proving that the tendency toward alcoholism is inherited. Our genes give us the tendency toward addiction and with the right societal and environmental conditions, we become addicted. Perhaps alcohol provides more euphoria for alcoholics than other people obtain from alcohol. This would relate to how the brain responds. One person can pick up a few drinks and find euphoria. After just a few sips, another person, even in the same family, can just become nauseated.

It is very interesting to mention here that the prefix "EU," as in euphoria, means normal. Therefore, as we have already seen, the potential addict and co-dependent feel so low that the drink, drug or other object of addiction just brings them *up to* what a normal person feels without that drink.

Another possibility is that alcoholics have a congenital inability to enjoy ordinary life pleasures. Dr. Sydney Cohen in his book *The Chemical Brain* suggests that they have an inborn deficiency of receptors at the reward center or a deficiency of dopamine neurons at those reward centers. It is possible that the alcoholic has inherited a central nervous system with a low tolerance for frustration, stress or anxiety. Therefore their suffering is greater, even though their existence does not seem more stressful.

This predisposition to alcoholism might also be due to genetic variations in neurotransmitter release and receptivity.

It is also possible that people have a difference of endorphin levels and, therefore, a wider variety of pain thresholds. It is possible that addiction proneness can be inherited and would manifest itself by a lower ability to endure stress or effective disorders. (1)

Many studies have shown that specific hormones are released when you drink and drug. The "high" reward comes more quickly with some drugs than others. They all have a profound effect on the nervous system, offering relief, rush, warmth and/or pleasure, depending on the drug.

Intoxication can serve one for sleep and relief of anxiety. At a recent talk, Enoch Gordis, Director of the National Institute of Alcohol Abuse and Alcoholism, said that the toxic consequences of alcoholism and all other addictions can be medical, surgical, psychological, social, financial, spiritual and legal. He says that alcoholism is the Number One drug problem in the United States.

If we look at the following list of the temporary, positive effects of this stimulant drug, alcohol, it is no wonder that anyone with low self-esteem would find relief in it. But these effects don't last and sooner or later, over a period of time, the negative effects take over.

Positive Effects	***Negative Effects***
Increased alertness	Irritability
Increased activity	Anxiety
Decreased appetite	Psychosis
Increased fight/flight reactions	Tremors
	Seizures
Euphoria/feeling happier	Isolation

Increased confidence	Brain damage
Feeling of well-being	Death

Why More Is Never Enough

By taking a drink or a drug, the effect is immediate and for the person who has always felt down or inhibited, the results of the first intake can lead the way to addiction. People addicted to sugar find the same relief in food.

Put all this together with what we already know about the endorphin systems closing down with stress and tension, add growing up in an alcoholic, other-addictive and/or dysfunctional home and we have a group of people prime for addictions, depressions, violence and *disease.*

Addictions

It is said that nature abhors a vacuum. When a rock has been removed from a lawn, the hole will eventually fill with weeds. When human beings feel empty, we search for something to take away that feeling, filling the space with something else to make us feel better.

My simple definition of co-dependency is that we reach outside of ourselves to feel better, rather than reaching within. In the most simplistic terms, we are co-dependent when we think we need people, places or things to feel all right. Co-dependents want to:

1. Feel more of what they feel in the moment if the feeling is pleasant.
2. Feel better than they do in the moment if the feeling is unpleasant.

We always want more. We never seem to have enough. Co-dependent people want to stop all pain and suffering. They want that to change *and right now.*

This is very normal. No one wants to feel pain, unhappiness or sorrow. Everyone would like to prolong good feelings but we get in trouble when we carry this too far. We get in trouble when we think that the only way we can feel good is through other people, places or things. We get in trouble when we think we cannot handle unpleasant situations and have to do something immediately to make things better. We are in trouble when we suffer because we do not have what we want or when we think we need it so much that we seek it even when we know that it is doing us harm.

Addiction is when we pursue that which produces a mood change to the point of being out of control. When we cannot stop.

The alcoholic or drug addict has a mood change when they use a chemical in the form of alcohol or drugs. When a person continues to use alcohol or drugs while knowing that it is harming any part of their life, whether their job, finances, family, sex, health or friends, they are addicts.

Many experts believe that all addictions involve the compulsive pursuit of a mood change by engaging repeatedly in a process despite negative or destructive adverse consequences.

At first, addicts are not aware that they are addictive. They are just grateful that they feel good. They think they have found something wonderful to help them feel okay. At last! The relief is there!

Gradually it takes more and more of whatever is the chosen object to bring about these good feelings.

I remember myself that one or two drinks would make me "feel good" but at some point it became three and then four. And I began to get worried. Deep inside, I knew something was wrong, but I didn't dare speak of this fear until many years later. I knew my drinking would be watched more carefully. I was protecting my right to drink. I knew I needed to drink to get through a day.

Craig Nakken, in his book *The Addictive Personality: Roots, Ritual and Recovery,* has depicted a clear way of seeing the addict. He paints the picture of the addict struggling with two parts within the self. He calls them the Self versus the Addict, and develops the scenario for the painful and destructive battle that goes on in the mind. (2)

To produce a desired mood change, addicts engage in a particular object or event. They are "out of control and are aimlessly searching for wholeness, happiness and peace through a relationship with an object or event." (3)

He gives examples resulting in mood changes: the alcoholic picking up a few drinks, the food addict binging or starving, the addictive gambler watching football on TV after placing a few bets, the shoplifter stealing, the sex addict browsing in a pornographic bookstore and the addictive spender going on a shopping spree.

> Acting out is when an addict engages in addictive behaviors or addictive mental obsessions . . . It is a way to create certain feelings that causes an emotional and mental shift within the person. It is the shift that the addict desires. (4)

Imagine that the addict actually has two people living inside. One person is called the Addict. The other person is called the Self. The addict is struggling with these two people within. The struggle goes something like this:

"Should I? Will I? No! Yes! Do I act out or don't I act out?"

This struggle, this conversation back and forth, this indecision creates a great tension inside. First the addict feels *pain.* This leads to *feeling the need to act out.* This leads to *acting out,* which helps the addict start to feel better. This results in more *pain* resulting from the *acting out,* which in turn leads to *feeling the need to act out* and so on.

> The addictive ritual helps to ease the tension. When an addict is involved in a ritual, this conflict is momentarily over because a choice has been made. There is a sense of release. (5)

Nakken gives other examples of acting-out rituals: the alcoholic going in the package store, the gambler studying the racing form or the sex addict cruising the streets.

Loss of self-respect and self-confidence is caused by this acting out and giving in to the Addict within, which creates more pain.

The internal conflict begins with the Self and the Addict within. Any feeling that creates discomfort becomes a signal to act out. (6) There is then a decrease in the Self which causes an increase in the addictive personality.

Addicts are chasing control of their feelings. They think that if they make themselves feel better, they are in control. What they don't see is that they are using something outside of themselves, something that is, or ultimately will be, destructive.

In the early stages the addict feels a high; they feel alive and complete. Stage One is "euphoric recall" to the pleasure of acting out, which the addict continues to chase.

For the addict the mood change gives the illusion that the need has been met. (7) Later there is less pleasure but the addict now develops a delusional system and begins lying, cheating, and staying away from people who try to stop them.

The addict becomes more and more ritualized, using the addictive substance in the same way as the time before and in this they find great comfort. Rituals are based on consistency. First you do this and then you do that.

Going Back . . .

Even though it was many years ago, I'll never forget the last bottle that I ever bought . . . on March 9th, 1973. The reason that I remember this so clearly is that I wrote out my last check to a package store and I can see in my mind's eye the entire check made out to O'Brien's Package Store. It was for a quart of J&B scotch. (My last drink was actually Nov. 26, 1973, but that was cough medicine and that's another story.)

I had been sitting in a doctor's office waiting for my appointment. I was sober three weeks, the longest that I had gone without a drink for years. And I really wanted to drink.

I had been told that if I asked a power greater than myself to keep me away from a drink, it would work. And it had worked for three weeks. But that day I was exceptionally tense, nervous about the outcome of this doctor's visit and I was *intent* on drinking. I remember sitting there with clenched fists, saying to myself, "Okay, I'll ask for help. But I'll show them this won't work!"

Immediately after the appointment I drove across the street and bought a quart of scotch. I remember putting the bottle next to me on the seat of the car. I remember even patting it as if it were alive. There was a feeling of complete calm around me. I was not tense any longer. In fact, I did not even have to take a drink to relax. The decision was made. I was no longer in battle with myself. I didn't even have to drink it. It was next to me and I was at peace for the moment.

I drove home and went directly to the laundry room downstairs. I looked around to see if anyone could see me, took off the cap and held the bottle up to my lips, taking some fast gulps. The burning liquid poured down my throat and into my chest, and there was nothing else to think about. I had what I wanted. The battle for today was over. Tomorrow was another day. I wouldn't drink tomorrow. The battle would begin again tomorrow. Today was fine. Just fine.

Looking back at this scene, I can see that my *intention* was to drink. "I'll show them! Praying won't work for me!" I clearly showed that my intention was to drink and not get help. The decision was made. That was all I needed to feel better for that time. Just the knowledge that I would be drinking within the hour was enough for me to relax. The peace that I felt once the bottle was bought, showed the peace that came from the decision, again the intention. This decision could have killed me. By giving in to my addiction, I might not have had another chance. Later I learned to trust that a power greater than myself could and would, if asked, keep me away from that first drink.

Later, I chose to live.

Compulsions

Nakken believes that the Self always witnesses the addictive ritual and is often sickened by what it is forced to watch and participate in, but it is being held captive by the power of the disease. (8)

Timmen Cermack, well known for his early work in the Adult Children of Alcoholics movement, describes *compulsions* as follows:

> "Compulsivity is a primary defense process. The object of a compulsion is of secondary importance and often changes over time . . . The internal dynamic is always the same: A struggle between two poles, one "inside" and one "outside." The person's identity is connected to resisting the impulse, while the impulse itself is experienced as an alien force. The resulting high drama distracts the person from unwanted feelings, which usually have nothing to do with whatever compulsion is occupying center stage . . .
>
> "There is a surge of adrenaline. An intense build up of emotions specific to the compulsions occurs . . . a feeling of inevitability takes over. Eventually they stop resisting the compulsion, and this is followed by a temporary sense of relief." (9)

Addictive rituals will ease this tension, for when an addict is involved in a ritual, this conflict is momentarily over. A choice has been made. There is a sense of release. (10)

The physical sensation begins with the thought, the idea of acting out. This is clear to see in the sex addict. Pat Carnes theorizes in *Out of The Shadows* that the addict's addictive process involves four steps:

1. Preoccupation
2. Ritualization
3. Compulsive sexual behavior
4. Despair.

In order to get relief from the despair, the addict returns to preoccupation with sex. In preoccupation, the addict gets into a trance or mood where the mind is completely engrossed with thoughts of sex. This creates an obsessive search for sexual stimulation. (11)

> "The addict's mood is altered as he or she enters the obsessive trance. The metabolic responses are like a rush throughout the body as adrenaline speeds up the body's functioning. Risk, danger and even violence are the ultimate escalators. One can always increase the dosage of intoxication. Preoccupation eventually buries personal pain of remorse or regret. The addict does not always have to act. Often just thinking about it brings relief." (12)

Dr. Benson, in *Your Maximum Mind*, paints what I think is a very easy to understand picture:

> "Over the years, you develop 'circuits' and 'channels' of thought in your brain. These are physical pathways which control the way you think, the way you act and often, the way you feel. Many times, these pathways or habits become so fixed that they turn into what I call 'wiring.' In other words, the circuits or channels become so deeply ingrained that it seems almost impossible to transform them. They actually become part of your brain. They are part of you." (13)

As we have seen, many experts believe that there is a genetic predisposition to addiction. This does not mean that if we are predisposed to addiction, we will become addicts. Many other factors come into play here, including family, society, how we are taught to handle stress, the amount of love and touch we are given, etc.

When we finally get into our addictive thinking, it does not go away by itself. As we learn to ask for help from a power greater than ourselves and from other people, and to work the tools of recovery, we will change our addictive thinking. As we continue to develop the stress-releasing, tension-relieving habit of talking about what is bothering us to a trusted sponsor, friend or therapist, our desire to escape via methods outside ourselves will be less and less powerful and felt less frequently. But for all of us there will still be times of tension and pain when our first thought will be a screaming *escape* into whatever it was we thought brought us relief in earlier times.

Know that these periods are completely human. Know that you are not necessarily doing anything wrong. In another section of this book you will learn about the powerful tool of *noting*.

Today I am on my spiritual path to recovery

What the caterpillar calls the end of the world,
the Master calls the butterfly.

Richard Bach

Going Back . . .

The scene is college, in the Rec room of my dormitory. The year is 1953. I am 17 years old and it is my freshman year.

Everyone is sleeping. It is 2:30 in the morning and I sit alone and struggle, pen in hand, over a spiral notebook, one of many notebooks that will follow me in my search for the truth, my many years of struggle, darkness, denial and pain. They will follow me until finally, blessedly, they follow me into the light of recovery, reality, purpose and love. I write this poem:

There is something I have to do . . .
An urge eating deep inside of me;
And until I find out what it is
I will never, never be free.

In the darkness of my thoughts
I'm lost.
I sink within my sins
In the struggle to know myself
And just where to begin.

Who is right?
Who is to say?
Why does God desert the few?
Why does God make good men suffer?
Who is right and
What is true?

R.F. 1953

I was lonely, paranoid, depressed and felt inferior to almost everyone. And yet, paradoxically, because of the prejudice I was taught in my family, I felt superior to a few. And I hid all this with a mask of deep and painful shyness, and an occasional air of confidence and superiority. This thin layer of superiority worked well to hide the depth of my feelings of inferiority. Much to my amazement, I was later to learn that my shyness and extreme self-consciousness were taken as snobbery by some.

Another scene 17 years later in the office of a psychiatrist. The year is 1971. I am 34 years old.

It is my first visit to a psychiatrist. I have finally come to the truth that I need help. I no longer can deny that my drinking is out of control. I cannot stop. I dare not stop. I suddenly remember the first two stanzas of the poem I wrote in college. I am now in deep depression and full of fear. I recite this poem to the inept doctor who knows nothing about alcoholism and is still arrogant enough to think that he can "cure" me with his wisdom and 31 varieties of pills.

"Try this red one. Oh, that didn't work? Then maybe the blue one. Or the yellow one. Or, wait! Here is a pink and green striped pill! That ought to do it! You can't sleep? Here is something for that. And you are shaking from too many pills? Take this! Take that!"

I am looking outside myself again for my answers. To the "authority," not yet knowing that I "author" my own truth, am my own authority.

And I tell him:

"I wrote this poem when I was 17.
And now I am 34.
Will I be the same at 51?"

I plead, I beg for help, for answers. And I get a new prescription. This time they are round, light blue pills. They are not to be used when eating chicken livers or drinking wine and champagne. Scotch is okay . . . probably. But you might get nauseated. Or faint . . .

6

The Heroine's And Hero's Journey

Wherever you are today is perfect.
You have been on a journey arriving right here,
right now in this moment in time and space.
You are here to make a new beginning on your
spiritual journey and to experience and accept
joy in your life. You are in a perfect place for
spiritual growth and change. Everything you have
done in your entire life has brought you to
this very moment and it is perfect.

Accept yourself just as you are. All of yourself.
Completely. Know that you are perfect
and let yourself feel the joy of that knowledge.

R.F. (1)

Imagine for a moment that

YOU ARE HERE

This is your past. ***This is your future.***

Know that the past cannot be changed.

You are right here now as a result of all that was, including your genes, circumstances at birth, heritage, culture, environment and your life's experiences.

We all had to do everything we did to bring us right here now. We could not have done it any differently. If we had known how to avoid the pain, we surely would have.

Imagine that you have been on a journey, as in truth you have. We have all been on a journey, walking on our own paths of life. We have been searching for healing. We have been searching for peace, truth and love.

For some, the journey is more difficult and painful than for others. For those people brought up in an alcoholic, drug dependent or dysfunctional home, their journey has had many more hazards than for those brought up with well-adjusted parents. For the future addicts and/or co-dependents, searching in unhealthy destructive ways to find peace, to put an end to our suffering, our lives have been full of such pain that at times we did not think we could endure another moment. When our addiction or obsession of choice stopped working for us, when we could no longer get the relief we so desperately sought, these times were the most painful of all.

To add to our burden we have carried sacks full of secrets, fears, guilt and shame. We have carried our own personal secrets. We have carried the secrets of our families. We have carried generations of secrets . . . memories of secrets kept deep within us, hidden by fear of discovery, fear of getting caught, fear of punishment, fear of further prejudice leading to more isolation and more pain. We all have carried with us fear of the unknown and the ultimate fear: fear of dying. All that we have carried with us from our past has blocked our energies and made us weak.

But there comes a time when the pain within us is the loudest voice we hear. There comes a time when something within us screams for release, for freedom. And we have to listen. We are forced to listen. We are brought to our knees by pain.

Our particular journey may have been slower than some and may have made us very tired and worn out . . . physically, mentally and spiritually. The tragedy is that many left their journey early in life, through accidents, suicide and sickness, without ever having found their path.

Many great stories and myths have told us for thousands of years, of the search and struggle of humankind for the meaning of life. They have lasted this long because they have touched a place deep within us, a place that we all are born with and share. The search for purpose and truth in our lives, for self-validation, comes from this place. Many of these stories relate heroic journeys of great suffering and pain. They tell of a giving up of all that is known, of an inner searching, a spiritual awakening and an ultimate liberation.

Stories and myths help us to understand that we are not alone in our struggle in this personal search and that this search itself is part of the natural flow of everyone's life. It is a natural part in the process of growing up and maturing. We all have to take this journey if we are to be whole, and find or fulfill our ultimate purpose. No one can tell us how to walk it if we are to find our own truth. We can have guides and teachers but ultimately the decisions are our own.

The Power Of Myths

In the book *We,* Robert Johnson tells us that myths have uncanny power to thrill us, to uplift us and to pull us out of the pettiness of our ego lives. If we learn to listen, a myth gives us specific psychological information and teaches us the deep truths of the psyche.

> A myth is the collective 'dream' of an entire people at a certain point in their history. (2)

Joseph Campbell, famous for his work in mythology, wrote in *The Hero With A Thousand Faces* that "the myth is the secret opening in which the inexhaustible energies of the cosmos pour into human cultural manifestation." (3) And he says further that "It has always been the prime function of mythology . . . to supply the symbols that carry the human spirit forward, in counteraction to those other constant fantasies that tend to tie it back." (4)

Campbell speaks of the four stages in the great journey of the archetypal hero or heroine:

1. The call to destiny. This is where we are set on our path of inquiry.
2. The great renunciation, the leaving behind of old patterns and habits. Beginning to see our lives in a new way.

3. The great struggle with all the forces of delusion.
4. The great awakening.

The Teacher's Manual of *A Course In Miracles* puts this another way. It says that peace cannot be ours until we go through six stages of development. (5)

1. ***A period of undoing.*** It seems as if things have been taken away. This is really a period where we are recognizing the lack of value in the things that we thought were important. There are changes in our external circumstances.
2. ***A period of sorting out.*** We must make a decision about all things as to whether they help or hamper us. We will find that most of the things once valued no longer help us in new situations as we grow. Here it is hard to give things up because we think we might need them.
3. ***A period of relinquishment.*** Here we give things up but it feels like a sacrifice. We still do not know that we are giving up something valueless. Where we have anticipated grief, we find happiness and lightheartedness. Where we have thought something was being asked of us, we find a gift instead.
4. ***A period of settling down.*** This is a quiet time and we rest in reasonable peace. It is a time to consolidate learning. It is a time to give up what you don't want and keep what you do.
5. ***Another period of unsettling.*** A new state will take a long time to reach. All judgment must be put aside and we must ask only for what we need.
6. ***Finally a period of achievement.*** We learn to consolidate. Tranquility is the result. Real peace is ours.

When you give up what the ego covets
and choose to accept what God freely gives, you will find
what you have never lost: the Self you are.

Robert May

The Story Of Moses

I would like to share the story of Moses with you because through the years it remains a beautiful example of a spiritual journey. The story of Moses has been told, retold and passed down through hundreds of generations. When we look at this story, we can compare the liberation of one group of people with our own personal liberation. Robert May, an author, teacher and student of Robert Johnson, tells us in his book *Physicians Of The Soul* that the story of Moses is the greatest liberation story ever told. (6)

May says the story of Moses is an allegory of the struggle of every person to escape his or her personal bondage and to become liberated.

Historians place this first "exodus" back in 1850 B.C., when Abraham came from Ur to Canaan, the Land of Promise. Abraham was the father of Isaac, who was the father of Jacob. Jacob was later renamed Israel, which means "he who struggles with the Lord." Israel fathered 12 sons who became the founders of the 12 tribes of Israel.

Many generations later, somewhere around the 13th century B.C., a new Pharaoh enslaved the Israelites. He used them as slave labor to build the splendid cities of the Pharaoh.

As the story goes, when Moses saw one of his people being beaten by an Egyptian, he killed the Egyptian and hid his body in the sand. The Pharaoh then ordered his soldiers to kill Moses. Instead Moses fled to the city of Midian, where he settled and married Zipporah when he was 40 years old.

One day while tending his flock on Mount Horeb, Moses saw a bush which, although totally engulfed in flames, was not burning. Then Moses heard the voice of the Lord tell him not to look at Him. Moses turned away and the Lord told Moses that He had seen the affliction of his people and that He had heard their cry.

He said that he intended to deliver them out of the land of their oppressors to a land "flowing with milk and honey," to the land of the Canaanites. And He told Moses that he must go to the Pharaoh and that He would be with him.

In spite of his fear, Moses and his brother Aaron presented themselves to the Pharaoh and said, *"Thus saith the Lord, the God of Israel: Let my people go, that they may hold a feast unto Me in the wilderness."*

The Pharaoh said he did not know who this "Lord" was, and he would not let the people go.

Moses begged:

"Let us go, we pray thee, three days' journey into the wilderness, and sacrifice unto the Lord our God; lest He fall upon us with pestilence or with the sword."

But the Pharaoh increased the burdens of the people, withholding the straw they needed to make bricks, while still requiring them to fulfill the same quotas.

Moses felt he had failed, so he went back to where he had encountered the Lord. God assured Moses that He was still with him. He told him to return to the Pharaoh to say that the Lord would visit a series of 10 plagues upon the Egyptians unless they let Moses' people go. The Pharaoh continued to resist until finally all the first born of the Egyptians were slain by the "Angel of Death." The grief of the Egyptians was so great that the Pharaoh finally relented and told Moses to take his people and go.

Full of faith, Moses took his 600,000 people with their belongings and their flocks and followed the path the Lord had chosen. When they reached the raging waters of the Red Sea, the Pharaoh changed his mind and ordered his army after them to recapture them. When they heard that, the people were afraid and told Moses that it was better to be alive in slavery than to die in the wilderness.

May compares this reaction with the security that people prefer rather than the scary risk of freedom. He writes that the Egyptians were closing in on the people and that many of them must have felt, "Why did you rock the boat, Moses? We could have lived in comfortable slavery."

How many of us have stayed in situations that enslaved us, not having the courage to risk leaving for the unknown? We didn't want to rock the boat, no matter how painful and destructive it was in that boat. How many of us have stayed in abusive relationships, continued destructive habits, given others power over us, swallowed toxic drugs, overate or starved ourselves, afraid that we could not survive otherwise?

Moses, with great faith, *"Stretched out his hand over the sea; and the Lord caused the sea to go back by a strong east wind all night, and made the sea dry land, and the waters were divided."* Then the Children of Israel crossed over the Red Sea. As the Egyptians tried to pursue them, the sea closed in and they were drowned.

When the Israelites took a leap of faith and crossed the Red Sea to freedom, they found themselves in barren wilderness or desert where they spent the next 40 years wandering from place to place. It was a hard and barren time, but it was not a wasted time. This was the period when Moses was given the Holy Law — the 10 Commandments. May says that we all receive our "Holy-Law-in-the-desert" period which is a time of intense clarity.

Moses then led his people to Mount Sinai where he was told by the Lord he alone should come to the top of the mountain and that his people should remain below. Here he communed with the Lord for 40 days and 40 nights.

(Centuries later the Buddha sat under the Bodhi Tree for 40 days and 40 nights in order to find a way to end world suffering. Six hundred years after that, Jesus Christ also fasted in the desert for 40 days and 40 nights, praying for guidance and readying himself for the trials to come.)

Moses brought the people to the threshold of their Promised Land and before he died, he said to his people:

"I have set before thee life and death, the blessing and the curse; therefore choose life . . ."

May says, "The goal, then, of each of the World Teachers was to instruct us human beings in exile on the way home . . . Home is "the Tao," "the Promised Land," "the Kingdom," "Nirvana," "Brahman" or "Allah." Home is the Source.

He shows us the four steps we take before we get to step five, which is freedom:

1. Compliance or submission to the authority system in question.
2. Rebellion.
3. Self-justification.
4. Action through faith.

First the Jews stayed and were slaves, not realizing they had a choice. When Moses saw a man being beaten, he rebelled and killed the guard.

May compares this to our personal freedom. When we try to break away from the Pharaohs of our life, "they tend to retaliate with increased burdens and harsh punishments. Pharaoh tends to become more, not less, oppressive when you announce to him your wish to become free."

Overbearing parents and school authorities sometimes inhibit our natural instincts and suppress our egos. Too much repression inhibits normal sexuality, aggression, self-assertion, independence and autonomy.

Partners and spouses often try to hold on tighter, become more oppressive, and use more cunning tactics if the mate tries to leave.

Moses hit his bottom when he saw the Israelite being beaten and he said he was not going to take it anymore. May compares the slavery of the Israelites to our loss of freedom and loss of our own way when we are not treated with respect.

Before the Israelites crossed the Red Sea to freedom, they found themselves in a barren wilderness where they spent 40 years wandering. When Moses' people had to go through their struggles to get to the promised land, they tried to justify going back by saying that at least they had their needs met when they were slaves.

Although it was a hard and barren time, it was not wasted time because the people were given the 10 Commandments to guide them in their struggle to live according to God's direction and to pass on to those still suffering in the world.

We do not have to even risk the adventure alone . . .
for the heroes of all time have gone before us;
the labyrinth is thoroughly known; we have only to follow
the thread of the hero path. And where we had
thought to find an abomination, we shall find a God;
where we had thought to slay another,
we shall slay ourselves; where we had thought to
travel outward, we shall come to the center of our own
existence; where we had thought to be alone,
we shall be with all the world.

Joseph Campbell

Like the Israelites, we receive our Holy Law as well in this period of our lives, a period of intense clarity when we have suffered all we can and must choose another path.

Each Spiritual Leader — Moses, The Buddha, Jesus and Bill Wilson — had an "awakening" that brought their people out of bondage. They developed a moral code for the purpose of ending suffering. Each of these spiritual leaders found a path on which to bring their people home.

Going Back . . .

I was a junior in college. It was 1956, still years away from the time when the hippies poured in droves into San Francisco, years away from Woodstock and the Beatles, Women's Lib and the Peace Movement and years away from students thinking they could make a difference in the world. These were still the years when a nice girl went to college to "catch a man," raise a family, experience the "together life" and want for nothing more.

It was the time when a nice girl put her family's happiness before her own, pleased her husband and if she was better than him in any way, she didn't show it for fear she would lose him. If a woman "had" a husband, children, a home and two cars, she "had everything." There was "something wrong with her" if she wasn't happy.

This was before Betty Friedan's *Feminine Mystique* told me I was okay to want more and gave me permission to be more than a housewife, a mother and a wife, without guilt.

I told my parents that I wanted to go to California after college. Looking back now, I really don't know why I was attracted to California, whether it was the sunshine or the wonderful spirit of life that I imagined. Maybe it was the fact that it was far away from my family and a chance to be independent. At any rate, I told them and it was like dropping a bomb shell.

Their response came as a complete surprise and shook me to the core. My mother seemed to go into an instant depression. She became very sad, very down and very small. She seemed to shrink before my eyes. She did not say a word. My father took me aside and said that if I went to California, there was a good chance my mother would get bleeding ulcers like her sister and die.

My mother was a very healthy woman at that time. She never had ulcers. My aunt, although she did have bleeding ulcers had not died from them. In fact, she went on to live over 30 more years. But just the threat that my mother might die as a result of my actions was enough to keep me at home. It was enough to hold me tightly and to make me live in the same state that my parents lived in for the next 30 years of my life. It kept me long after my mother died, over 20 years later.

My father continued to burden me with shame and guilt. Robert May says that Pharaohs tend to become more, not less, oppressive when you announce your wish to become free.

Years earlier when I had locked myself into my bedroom so that my father would not beat me, my mother gave me a similar message. My father would be pounding the door, yelling for me to open it. My mother would say, "Ruth, open the door or your father will have a heart attack." I was afraid that he would beat me if I opened the door. I was afraid that he would have a heart attack if I didn't. Not a good choice, either way! But it certainly gave me the message of my power over his life or death.

Now, again, I was being told I had power over the life of my mother. As I did not have the strength, courage, independence, maturity or wisdom to leave, I told him I would never mention California again. I did not have the courage to risk rocking the boat.

A few days later I received a three-page letter from my father that basically asked what was wrong with me. He said that what made this country great was its independent spirit. He had always admired that characteristic in me. He admired the fact that I fought back and did what I wanted to do. He wrote, "What do you mean, you'll never mention California again? Where's that old spunk that you're known for?"

Too many mixed messages! Too much of a burden! I can still feel the heavy sigh I released when I folded the letter in thirds and returned it to its envelope. I can still feel my shoulders stoop and see the room gray and dull as if it were yesterday. I never did mention California again to him and I didn't get there until much later. But I carried that resentment with me for many years. I blamed him for not letting me go to California! I was 22 years old, thinking I was very independent and yet I still needed permission to leave my block.

Years later my mother came down with Hodgkins Disease. With treatment, she was lucky enough to go into remission for the next five years.

Those years were very painful and full of crises, turmoil and miracles for me. I finally (and gratefully) reached my own bottom with my disease of alcoholism. What followed was another very dark personal period that existed side by side with a bright and joyous time. I survived the most painful and agonizing decision to leave my children with their father and leave my marriage of 15 years. I lost the fight for joint custody of my children. I lost all financial assets. But I finally became free to be me.

My poor mother could not handle all her pain. She withdrew from friends and family, just going to work and coming home. She was deeply concerned for my children. And she was tearful for her job because she lived with all the tapes from her own formative years. In her mind she heard her own tapes asking, "What will people think of me if they find out what my daughter has done? Will they think that I have done wrong?" The truth is that my mother had done nothing wrong. She loved us the best that she could. She gave us all that she had.

Subsequently, she began to age quickly and developed cancer of the stomach during the next year. Within two months of the appearance of cancer, she was dead.

My father blamed me and hated me for her death. The next year I received a long and morbid 13-page letter from him, blaming her death on me. Intellectually I knew that my mother had died from her own reactions to life's circumstances.

Facilitated by her withdrawal, her fear and her closing up, the disease ate away at her. I knew that it didn't have to be that way for me and I knew I could no longer live my life in fear of someone else's death. I knew again how much I must hold on to everything that I had learned, that I could not take on the burden of this blame.

Far from achieving what he intended, my father's letter finally began to set me free at a much deeper level. I wrote back that he should never say those things to me again. But it has taken many more years of work to forgive him for his accusations.

Years later I celebrated my fifth sober anniversary in California, an independence and a victory hard won. I have a picture of me standing in front of a sign that says:

WELCOME TO CALIFORNIA

I had finally made it! I, too, had come home!

7

THE HUNDREDTH MONKEY SYNDROME

When enough of us are aware of something, all of us become aware of it.

Ken Keyes, Jr.

In 1985 a professor stimulated my imagination by sharing with our class the phenomenon of the hundredth monkey.

Scientists had been observing monkeys in the wild for 30 years. In 1952 on the island of Koshima they provided monkeys with sweet potatoes which they dropped in the sand. The monkeys liked the taste of the potatoes but found the dirt unpleasant.

An 18-month-old female name Imo washed the potatoes in a nearby stream. She taught this trick to her mother and her playmates, who then taught their mothers. The scientist watched as various monkeys began washing their sweet potatoes. Between 1952 and 1958 all the young monkeys learned to wash the sandy sweet potatoes to make them more palatable.

Soon all the adults who imitated their children were washing their potatoes, while other adults kept eating dirty sweet potatoes. It is not known how many monkeys washed their sweet potatoes this way. As the story is told, the scientists made an assumption that perhaps as many as 99 monkeys washed their potatoes this way. One day the 100th monkey learned to wash potatoes. Suddenly almost every monkey began washing potatoes before eating them.

The added energy of this hundredth monkey had somehow created an ideological breakthrough.

But more amazing, it was observed by the scientists that the habit of washing sweet potatoes had jumped over the sea, as colonies of monkeys on other islands began washing their sweet potatoes.

Author Ken Keyes, Jr., in his book *The Hundredth Monkey** writes that when a certain critical number achieves an awareness, this new awareness may be communicated from mind to mind. (1) When a limited number of people know something in a new way, it remains the conscious property of only these people. But there is a point at which if only one more person tunes in to a new awareness, a field is strengthened so that the awareness is picked up by almost everyone.

Many events that have occurred before and since that time illuminate this as truth. People all over the world, within days, weeks and months of each other, have taken strong stands insisting upon their right to freedom. It is as if the majority of the people of this universe have all been reading the same book. Some have read it slowly. Some a bit more quickly. But they have all come in their own time to the page that says:

"You have a right to freedom."

As of the moment of this writing, many nations of the world are uniting against Iraq's invasion of Kuwait in the Middle East. This is the first time in history that so many nations have joined together to restore freedom to another nation.

We have not gone far enough but we are on the path. More and more people are aware of what needs to be done and taking action. Yes, there is still suffering. Fighting is still going on in some parts of the world. It is said now that 40,000 children die

---

**The Hundredth Monkey*, Ken Keyes, Jr., Vision Books, 790 Commerical Avenue, Coos Bay, Oregon 97420. This book is not copyrighted. Ken Keyes asks that we reproduce it and distribute it in as many languages as possible, to as many people as possible.

each day of starvation, and it is predicted that AIDS will take hundreds of thousands of lives if a cure is not found.

Millions of people are demanding personal freedom in their countries. Governments are being forced to listen. The Berlin Wall has finally come down. Poland, Czechoslovakia, Romania and East Germany, have new forms of government. Changes are suddenly happening that are bringing people to personal freedom.

Awareness has finally grown to a universal level where we are at least aware that we have raped our own lands. On one hand things are slowly changing.

On the other hand, poverty and homelessness have reached new heights in the United States. Drugs and alcohol plague our youngsters, along with poor education and illiteracy. I travel a lot, speaking around the country, and when I put on the 11 o'clock news, it is often difficult to know what city I am in. It could be Boston, with two killed in a jealous rage, or Dallas where an 11-year-old boy was shot by mistake while he was riding his bike home from school, and on and on and on.

There is still too much sexual and physical abuse, gang wars, drug wars, crime, neglect, illiteracy, suppression of women, Jews, Blacks and other minorities.

Yes, the world is full of pain and suffering, starvation and fear, terrorism, wars, poverty and hopelessness. But it is changing.

People everywhere are experiencing Spiritual Awakenings and coming home.

Going Back . . .

I felt messy and dirty. I had not taken more than one or two baths in the last week. My hair was stringy and oily. My clothes looked as if I had slept in them. As I walked out the door of my middle class suburban home where three young children slept restlessly, guilt and shame filled my every pore. How could I leave my children for hours? But how could I not?

If I stayed home, I would die. But I was dying anyway.

The pain I felt inside was beyond anything I could bear another moment. I took another sip from the bottle in the brown paper bag and put it in the glove compartment. The familiar burning hit my throat with instant relief and I could feel the liquid warm my chest, my arms, and my torso down into my feet as I began to feel myself relaxing. I reached in my pocket for the very handy mints, in case I got stopped on the way.

By the time I had arrived at the meeting place, the scotch had worn off and the tension was back full force. I forced myself to go into the building. I expected to find drunks, derelicts and skid row bums. I kept my eyes down on the floor. Surprisingly the room was full of chatter and laughter.

I walked to the back of the room and introduced myself to the woman who was pouring coffee. She called over to a few young well-dressed, attractive women who came to meet me. They smiled and showed me to a seat.

Looking directly into my eyes they said, "Welcome. We know your pain. We have been there, too, and we have come to the other side of it. We are free of it. We are alcoholics. Welcome. If you have a problem with alcohol, you are in the right place."

I buried my face in my hands. But something moved deep inside me. I knew they were telling me the truth. I knew they had felt what I felt. I knew that whatever it was they had, I wanted it. I had been searching for it all of my life.

Finally I dared to look around. I saw that I was the dirtiest, most unkempt of all. Me with my college education and my business success. Me with my home in the suburbs and two expensive cars in the garage.

I looked at the smiling attentive faces, laughing with a speaker who shared things I did not think possible to tell anyone at all. I did not understand how they could laugh at anything so personal and painful. But they had something and I wanted it.

I knew I was home.

This and countless stories similar to it are told every day and every evening in the halls of 12-Step programs around the world. Whether the problem is alcohol or drugs, gambling or eating, sex or emotions, 12-Step programs have saved the lives of millions of people and brought them to a new level of happiness, contentment and peace.

There is a growing group of people who are getting better. These people suffered from oppression and depression, physical, mental and sexual abuse. They left their oppressors thinking they had a new answer, reaching out to follow the neon light of the addictions, obsessions and co-dependencies, thinking this was the way to their land of Milk and Honey.

These people had once been slaves, but after years of work on their recovery, having a Spiritual Awakening, and in order to remain well, they continue to pass on their messages to others who are still suffering. This is the only way they have been able to keep their freedom — by sharing it and passing it on to others who are still out there suffering.

Many other afflicted people have borrowed their "ten commandments" and adapted them to their own needs. They have found freedom. They have come home.

8

The 12-Step Movement

As a result of these 12 steps we have a Spiritual Awakening.

Bill Wilson

After years of suffering and losses, and unable to stop drinking for any length of time, Bill Wilson finally reached a point of absolute desperation. He experienced what he called a "spiritual awakening." To stay sober he then reached out in 1934 to another suffering alcoholic, Dr. Bob Smith of Akron, Ohio. In 1935 they combined the principles they were using to stay sober. This later became the basis of AA's 12 Steps of Recovery.

Bill Wilson said:

> "These were revolutionary and drastic proposals but the moment I fully accepted them, the effect was electric. There was a sense of victory, followed by such a peace and serenity as I had never known. There was utter confidence. I felt lifted, as if the great clean wind off a mountaintop blew through and through. God comes to most men gradually, but His impact on me was sudden and profound. (1)

I believe the Self-Help Movement, inspired by Alcoholics Anonymous (AA), is a powerful example of the power of this phenomenon of the collective unconscious.

Until 1935 most alcoholics were considered hopeless. Today millions of people are recovering and sober because of AA. Thousands of AA groups meet every day and night of the week in almost every part of the world and its literature is published in dozens of languages.

Since the founding of Alcoholics Anonymous, at least 60 other 12-Step programs have followed. They address other problems such as sex, overeating, gambling, overworking, overspending and child abusing, just to name a few.

Millions of active alcoholics became parents and brought up their children in trauma and dysfunction. These children grew up not knowing what was wrong with them. Most felt different, separate, alone. Many lived with deep suffering. They did not know how to cope with life on life's terms. Many thought they were crazy and that something was seriously wrong with them. These children were spiritually deprived.

In 1981 a new phenomenon stirred the souls of millions of these people. The characteristics they all had in common began to be identified and their pain took a new name: *Adult Children Of Alcoholics* (ACoAs). It happened as suddenly as the 100th Monkey Syndome. People began to get together and talk and share. They borrowed the 12-Steps of Alcoholics Anonymous and formed their own program. Therapists began to specialize in the treatment of ACoAs.

And still many other people were hurting. They did not necessarily come from alcoholic or drug-addicted homes. They came from homes that were dysfunctional in other ways. They were brought up by people who were filled with their own fear, shame and guilt, then passed it on to their children. They were brought up by overeaters, overspenders, overworkers, gamblers and sexual and physical abusers. These children were spiritually deprived as well.

In the mid-'80s yet another new phenomenon stirred the souls of millions more. Common characteristics were again identified and their personal pain took on a new name: *Co-dependency.* The 100th Monkey Syndrome was occurring again.

Getting together to talk and share, they too borrowed the 12-Steps of AA and formed their own program. Therapists began to specialize in the treatment of co-dependency. While

ACoAs and Co-dependents did not necessarily drink alcoholically or use drugs to change their moods, they did reach out to other people, places and things to feel better. Many had other addictions, compulsions and obsessions. They needed to reach outside of themselves to feel better.

My simple definition of co-dependency is reaching outside of ourselves to feel better, wanting more and more of what makes us feel good and resisting anything that makes us unhappy. We want to change the reality of our lives from the outside, not from the inside.

Co-dependency issues touch all of us as human beings. There are many good books, therapists, workshops and conferences that can help us with these and other issues mentioned.

Today a growing number of people are in recovery. Joy has begun to creep into our lives. We have taken the painstaking steps to freedom on the journey of recovery.

All the people in the world have been handed the gift of recovery. It is here for everyone. Now all of us can have the tools for a spiritual awakening. Now all of us can come home.

We have been in exile . . .
We are coming to the promised land . . .
We are coming back to ourselves . . .
We are coming home!

PART TWO

Feelings are chemicals that can kill or cure.

Bernie Siegel

9

The Power Of Recovery

To live with great wisdom and compassion is possible for anyone who genuinely undertakes a training of their heart and mind.

Jack Kornfield

Once we are on the path to recovery, we find there are many simple, powerful and healing methods we can use to be in charge of the flow of our endorphins, thus the flow of our feelings and our health. Tools are right at our fingertips, as close as our breath, our thoughts, our words . . . as close as our hearts. Our healing power extends to the people we include in our lives, our family and friends, our community, our colleagues and our support groups.

Where and how we live and work are all choices we can make for ourselves today. Even the way we dress, the colors we use and the way we relax are all things that need to be re-examined in the light of what we know now.

- Where are you going and what will you do when you get there?
- What are your assets?
- Your strengths?
- Your dreams?

As you get to know yourself better and make positive changes in your life, it will become clearer how you can use these powerful tools for change. As you become more and more willing to give up the destructive forces, such as addictions, co-dependency, fear and negativity, you will begin to be energized by the Healing Power Of Recovery.

Candace Pert, chief Biochemistry at the National Institute of Mental Health, sees the "body as the outward manifestation of the mind." In her view, the body and the brain are inseparable. She believes evidence that there are chemical messengers in the body as well as those in the brain. Some can be found in our intestines as well as our limbic systems (our "feeling brain"). Our feelings are not just in our brain but in our body. She says we should learn to trust our "gut reactions." Having a gut feeling about something is more than just a figure of speech. (1)

Power Of Words

I have always believed in the Power Of Words and have seen them work in my life and the lives of countless others. While still in college, I started a greeting card business that continued for 17 years. It was successful because it was a vehicle for people who could not express themselves in any other comfortable way. We all have an innate need to communicate with one another, to express ourselves and to share our feelings. So I created inspiring and loving messages in a light and humorous style. People could send a card that said "I Love You" and not feel embarrassed because the card said it for them.

I changed the focus of my cards to messages for recovery as I grew in my own recovery. I created another greeting card line while with Serenity, Inc., called Inspirations of Serenity and another called *Time For Joy* for Health Communications, Inc. I would watch people's reactions, see them smile or pause, relax or even cry at some of the different messages. I know that words *move* people from a place deep within. We are *touched* by words. They reach into our hearts.

We know that words and touch stimulate endorphins and actually change our moods. We know that from a place deep within our brain, thoughts are converted into biochemical and electrical messengers and spread throughout our body. They create the physical sensations we associate with feelings and emotions. (2)

Proof of the power that words have in our bodies is now clearer because of the use of brain scanning, which permits us to picture what is going on in our heads. PET (Pisitron Emission Tomography) is providing a "window into the brain" so that we can see the deficiency or excess of chemical messengers. It is now even possible to demonstrate the differences that feelings, such as love, intimacy and affiliation, rather than the need for power and domination, have on certain antibody levels. (3)

Steven Paul, chief of clinical neuroscience at NIMH, tells us that talk therapy is perhaps the most profound way to change body chemistry. (4)

Words Inspire

The word *inspire* comes from the Latin word meaning to breathe into.

> *Inspiration* is the "infusion or arousal within the mind of some idea, feeling or impulse, especially one that leads to creative action . . . Divine influence exerted upon the mind or spirit; the act of drawing in the breath; inhalation. *Inspire:* To insert an invigorative influence upon (a person); animate; stir: His words *inspired* the crowd. To move (a person) to a particular feeling, idea, etc.: It *inspires* me with hope. To arouse or create (a feeling, idea, principle, etc.); generate: to *inspire* fear." (5)

We *inspire* ourselves. Our very thoughts move us.

We are moved by the messages that we tell ourselves, to be positive or negative, healing or destructive. Our bodies respond with sickness or health.

It is very important that you listen to the way you talk to yourself. It is very important that you change any negative messages you give yourself.

Just as brain chemicals can change thoughts, so, too, can thoughts change the chemicals — and how well we feel and function.

Blair

Let yourself
F E E E E E E L
the effect of just one word.

Spend a few moments being still and let yourself F E E E L how powerful one word can be.

P E A C E

The Power Of Being Listened To:

Listening is a magnetic and strange thing, a creative force. The friends who listen to us are the ones we move toward, and we want to sit in their radius. When we are listened to, it creates us, makes us unfold and expand.

Karl Menninger

We need to be heard. After being told for so many years to be quiet, don't talk, don't tell the neighbors, we shut down. When it comes, the healing power of being listened to is felt immediately. It is as if a huge burden has been removed. Our stories must be told so that we can heal.

Twelve-Step programs are a wonderful place to begin to be listened to. Here we share our strength, hope and experience. Here is where we can identify with the feelings of others who have gone through the same thing that we have been through. People are there for us because they know the healing power of talking and being heard. They know it works because it has worked for them.

A 12-Step sponsor is someone who has experience in working the program and a person who you can identify with. A sponsor is a person who you can trust and with whom you can begin to share your story. Twelve-Step programs can help you in understanding sponsorship and finding a good sponsor.

A therapist or a religious person is another place where you can begin.

If you have a good friend or relative you can trust to take the time to be with you, consider that a gift.

The Power Of Sharing Our Secrets

The thoughts and experience that we have never shared, the thoughts and memories that sit inside of us like a boulder in the pit of our stomachs do us the most damage.

I remember the shame I used to feel about who I thought I was. I used to lie in bed in sweats, the sheets actually wet with the fear that someone would actually know me someday. I felt unworthy and "knew" there was something very wrong with me.

The first time that I ever shared deeply and honestly with someone I trusted, it took tons of weight off my shoulders. I had kept everything bottled up in me for my entire life. Until that time, I had not shared any of my deepest feelings for my entire 37 years. I was sure that she would think something was wrong with me. I experienced the exact opposite reaction. I was accepted. I was still liked. In fact, my sponsor went on to share some of her own personal story, letting me see how really human I was after all.

The Power Of Words And Touch

It has been shown that words and touch stimulate endorphins. We experience good feelings with a pat on the back or when we receive positive feedback after accomplishing something important. Some researchers say that these stimuli release a burst of endorphins in us. Endorphins make us feel good. Therefore children in a healthy family who receive words of praise and love, who are touched, held and affirmed as human beings, develop a natural flow of endorphins and a natural sense of well-being.

This psychobiological process has been programmed into us at a very early age. With it we become dependent early in our lives on endorphin stimulation to maintain a normal emotional and psychological state. (6)

Talking and touching are forms of "environmental enrichment" that we can use to change the internal chemical and neurogical environment in ways conducive to healing and growth. (7)

As an example of this process, I have always been fascinated by the Kennedy family. Rose Kennedy was the mother of one son who became President of the United States, another son who became Senator of Massachusetts and a third son who became Attorney General of the United States and Senator from New York state. She said that each person feels important in families when they realize that they are part of something . . . a bigger mission. Her children were affirmed and encouraged and all of them grew to be valued individuals who worked hard on behalf of their fellow men and women.

It is important to look at all the messages that made us feel "less than" the Kennedys. It's important to change those messages *today*.

The Power Of Feelings And Thoughts

Our thoughts and perceptions can push buttons by releasing various neurochemicals. The way we define our experiences can affect cell receptors. We produce stress hormones from an overly negative view of problems. These stress hormones produce changes in cell receptors for serotonin, a neurotransmitter that plays an important role in modifying psychic and physical pain. (8)

When we hold on to negative thoughts, such as anger and resentments, we have an inappropriate production of body chemicals that are actually dangerous when present in the wrong proportions. Embracing anger prompts the manufacture of high voltage chemicals of the body, such as adrenaline, noradrenaline, ACTH and cortisone. These are the chemicals that we need for fight-or-flight reactions when we are in real danger. They damage us physically when we do not release them.

When we have this overproduction of adrenaline, we get contractions in the muscles of the neck and head which lead to tension headaches. Other chemicals cause the heart to pound heavily and cause many stomach diseases.

Countless tests and experiments have proven that our minds are very powerful and our thoughts are connected to our feelings. Our thoughts and our feelings trigger chemical alterations in our bodies. Chemicals are released or repressed thus affecting our health.

Worry is an excellent example of negative imagery because when we worry, we set off the fight-flight response and our body becomes prepared for the worst. (9)

But worry can be changed by positive thoughts and affirmations.

The Power Of Perception

Imagine that a football game is going on. The Eagles and the Lions are playing for a world championship. The Eagles come from your state; therefore, you are rooting for them. In fact, you have even made a $2.00 side bet with a friend. You are home watching the game on television and the score is 28-7, with only three minutes to go and the Eagles are ahead. Imagine how you might be feeling. Excited! Elated! Happy! Victorious!

Now imagine the exact same scene on the screen in the home state of the Lions. A fan watching the same scene at the same moment knows that the game cannot be won in the time remaining. This fan is dejected, down and sad. Maybe even angry.

The same game, the same moment, a different perspective. Two people watching from two sets of circumstances with two different expectations or desires in mind.

Both brain chemistry and structure are affected by the way that we experience our environment. (10)

Mental states . . . thoughts, attitudes, moods . . . cause changes in the brain cells and their activity, affecting the nerve endings that release chemical transmitters. The neurons change their signals in the brain and the body as they respond to our perceptions. (11)

When you change how you look at a problem, i.e., as setbacks instead of catastrophes, the neurotransmitter disturbance appears to be relieved. By the way we define situations, we call forth inappropriate chemical and nervous system reactions. (12)

The Power Of Beauty

There is recent evidence about the effect on us when we are moved by music, the beauty of a sunset or a work of art. (13) We can actually feel thrills, goosebumps tingling from something that we observe through our senses. It is said that our endorphins are stimulated and we can experience physical pleasure when we listen to music.

Studies have show that when given naloxone, a synthetic drug that antagonizes and blocks certain parts of our brain, people were found to have less reaction, less chills up their spine when listening to their favorite passages of music. (14)

We feel a physical reaction to a sensual experience. Certainly sex is a most obvious example. We can see, hear, smell, touch or taste something that reminds us of sex and our body will respond.

The Power Of Tears

Ornstein and Sobel tell us that crying "cleans the mind" and that researchers are examining tears for endorphins, ACTH, prolactin, and growth hormone, all of which are released by stress. (15)

The Power Of Community

When we find people like ourselves, we relax. We feel comfortable. A sense of belonging is important for all of us. Mazlow placed the need to belong fourth in his hierarchy of needs, right after food, personal safety and protection.

When the early immigrants came to this country, they formed ghettos so that they would not feel isolated and alone.

Self-help groups fulfill this role in recovery. People find others like themselves who have shared their experiences and now are getting well.

Ornstein and Sobel say that our early dependency on other people is basic to the evolution of the brain. Our social nature links us fundamentally to others throughout our lives. When these links are strained or ruptured, the health consequences are profound.

The Healing Power Of Love

The effects of love can be measured. An unloved infant will have retarded bone growth and may even die. An infant who is stroked and caressed grows normally. The emotional environment we create within our bodies can activate mechanisms for destruction or repair.

Love is something we feel. Love opens our hearts. Love is the connection, the energy, between one human being and another human being. Love is so powerful it can change people's lives forever. People have given up jobs, families, wealth, power, thrones, and even their lives for love. Others have found new jobs, family, wealth and have begun brand new ways of life.

When my oldest daughter, Debbie, was two years old, she stood on the corner of our block to wait for the ice cream truck. I stook back a bit, giving her the space to take this grown-up step. I watched with awe, marveling at her little hand holding out a single dime, a beautiful look of innocence and trust on her face. I was so struck with the miracle of life and how this little human being had grown to this point of independence at that moment, knowing exactly what she wanted and waiting for it to come to her. I felt her sweetness and her innocence and I thought my heart would burst with joy and love as my eyes filled with tears of happiness.

Five years later my son, Bob, was sitting at the dinner table, tears streaming down his face. His father and I had been very open with our children about the facts of life. Recently Bob and I had been planting a garden. He was now in the third day of school. He had learned that he had limitations with his reading. He went to school thinking he could read everything and was exposed to reading that was beyond his ability. He was heart-broken. He said that he could never be a father. He could never plant the seeds. He couldn't read the instructions on the package, so he wouldn't know how to plant the seeds.

I remember feeling my heart open with love and compassion as I rose from my chair and went to comfort him, assuring him that he would know what to do when he was ready and that his were a different kind of seeds. The sweetness of his innocence and goodness brought tears to my eyes and I hugged him and cried with him.

Three years later, when my youngest daughter, Judy, was in the first grade, I attended a song festival at her school. I remember it being a dark night for me, a difficult time. I was just reaching the end of my drinking and was in a deep depression. I was only there because I had to be there for my daughter, but did not feel emotionally or physically up to sitting through the evening.

All the six-year-olds were on the stage, dressed in their best clothes from ties and jackets to ruffles and bows. The children sang out "What The World Needs Now Is Love, Sweet Love" in the sweet, innocent, uninhibited voices that only children have. I felt as if my heart woke up. I listened with all my being. I became very aware that I had not felt this way since Debbie held her hand out with her dime, since Bobby hurt so much because he thought he couldn't be a father. I knew my heart had closed down, my soul had dried up. My own disease had almost removed my ability to feel love. Tears streamed down my face. I was so grateful to be alive, to feel life, to feel love. I was so grateful for my children.

10

THE POWERFUL FREEDOM OF NOTING AND VOLITION

There are two kinds of suffering: the suffering that leads to more suffering and the suffering that leads to the end of suffering. If you are not willing to face the second kind of suffering, you will surely continue the first.

Achaan Chah

I want to share with you some very powerful tools that have changed my life. They work to clear our negativity and transpose it to positive energy. They work to help us to see where we are stuck and show us how we can move through these places. These tools began working for me when I began my own recovery from alcoholism, which eventually led to the writing of my first book, *The Journey Within, A Spiritual Path to Recovery*. I have been developing and refining these theories ever since, and sharing them in workshops and retreats throughout the country.

The letters I receive tell me that these tools are working in the lives of those who are using them, turning suffering into joy. They can also turn addiction and obsessions into freedom, resentments and anger into love. They can also change *your* life.

One common ground for all human beings is our ability to feel. We hurt and we suffer. We desire love and understanding. We want to be touched, to be held. We want to be safe.

Another common ground is that we all want to avoid pain. As we have seen, we do that in a variety of ways. Some shut down feelings. They don't feel at all or aren't in touch with their feelings. This often happens when they experience great shock or trauma in their lives. Others ignore feelings and develop denial systems, such as fantasies, physical sicknesses, chemical dependencies, over- or under-eating and a long string of compulsions and obsessions, including co-dependency. Using all these, they try to feel better so that they do not have to deal with their pain.

But remember that when we don't want to deal with any feelings or be in the reality of the moment, we shut down the very body chemicals that make us feel good. We put them out of commission.

Just because we are not dealing with pain and have developed a denial system does not mean that the pain isn't there. It comes out in unhealthy ways, keeping us from growing emotionally, physically and spiritually. It is a massive block that keeps us from being the best that we are.

The world is in a drug war because of this denial system. There is murder and crime in our streets because of this denial system. Children are not getting the care and love that they need to grow up to be healthy, contributing members of society. Countries, religions, groups, neighborhoods, clubs and gangs, families and individuals fight each other because of our denial systems.

We chase happiness to the point of self-destruction. It is as if we are afraid of the darkness. We only want to see the sunshine and cannot accept that night is a part of the natural cycle. We want fun without the responsibility. We demand freedom at any price. We think we can have our harvest without planting the seeds and plowing the fields. We want to feel good at any cost.

But the price is too high.

We only want to stop the pain.

To be part of the group . . .

To just be liked.
To be like everyone else.
To forget the past.
To feel peaceful and happy.

We block our truth. We hide from others and from ourselves. We live in denial. We blame others. When we do feel at all we live in guilt, shame, anger or pain. Or rage. Or hopelessness and despair. We lose the very thing that we are trying to find in the process: ourselves.

What I am about to present is not new. It is as old as the Buddha and Christ and Moses. I am just shining it under a new light. I am spotlighting it under the light of today, to bring light to the corners where pain and suffering live. We need in this way to open the closets where we hide the secrets that kill us and erase the shadows of alcohol and drugs, obsessions, compulsions and other addictive behaviors.

It can save the country. It can save the world. But first and foremost, it can save your life.

Volition

One day I was listening to a tape by Joseph Goldstein on meditation and I suddenly felt as if I were walking through an important new door into bright sunlight. He spoke of the moment of volition. He told me to find that important moment between the breathing in and the breathing out, and between the breathing out and the breathing in . . . the moment when nothing happens. He said that moment is one of the most important moments in our lives. That moment teaches us to control our impulses.

I had earlier attended a meditation class taught by Larry Rosenberg, another meditation teacher. He showed us that we do not have to give in to our itches or our body's desire to move just because our body tells us to move or scratch.

Imagine that you have an itch on your left arm. It takes less than a second for that itch to transmit the message to your brain that it wants to be scratched. In that same split second your brain sends a message to your right hand to scratch the itch on your left arm. It would still be another split second before your right arm would move to scratch your left arm.

This is the moment of choice.
This is the moment of volition.
This is the moment when we can learn to be in charge.

We do not have to give in.

We can make the decision not to scratch. And by bringing our full attention to the itch, it will go away without being scratched.

This is an important moment. Notice it! Because it is not all about itches but about giving into urges of all kinds. It is about letting impulses, compulsions and obsessions run our lives and eventually destroy us.

It is giving in to the urge for the ice cream sundae when we are addicted to sugar. It is the "just one" cigarette or scotch or bet. It is reaching out for the telephone to make a call that you know will prolong a destructive relationship. It is staying another night with a person who has abused you, thinking that if you can just find a way to act differently, then this time, this time will be different.

We All Want What We Want When We Want It

Most people want immediate gratification. Most people want what they want when they want it. We are a society that wants and expects immediate gratification. A large part of this is because often most of us did not get our needs met and we still do not trust that we ever will. We are afraid that there will never be enough for us and we want to make sure that we take it when we can.

We Want It Now!

It is easy to say that we can deprive ourselves tomorrow. We'll just do it or have it or eat it one more time! And we rationalize that we deserve it because we were deprived for so long when we were young.

How can we get over the urge, the desire, the compulsion?

Meditation is a wonderful tool that goes far beyond bringing us peace for the 20 or 30 minutes that we are sitting and meditating. During this time, we are becoming disciplined. We are training ourselves to guide our attention where we want it. As we continue to practice bringing attention to our breathing, we are learning to bring awareness to what is going on in the moment. As we do this, we learn from each moment.

One of the first times I experienced how this could work for me is a good example of what happens. I had taken a meditation course one night a week for ten weeks. The format of each session was the same every week. As we entered a large room, we got into a comfortable sitting position on the floor and meditated. The instructor then came in and meditated with us. After 20 minutes, he struck a brass bowl with a small carved piece of wood, creating a gentle ringing tone to mark the end of meditation.

Later I signed up for his advanced class, but was out of town for the first evening. I entered the room the second week, sat down as usual, and began meditating. After a while I was sure that 20 minutes must be over. I continued to meditate, wondering what was happening. My body began to ache and I wanted it to be over. I wanted to move. I wanted to change positions. Soon voices in my head began screaming, "When is he going to stop us? When is he going to ring the bell?" I thought I couldn't take it another second! Yet I sat there with every part of my body joining the screaming that was going on in my mind.

Finally he rang the brass bowl. I was filled with relief, frustration and anger. Because I had missed the first class, I had not known that the new meditation time had been stretched to 45 minutes!

I shared all that was going on with me and the instructor said, "Wonderful! How did it feel to be so impatient? How did it feel to want to move and yet not give in to your body? How did it feel to be angry at me and want me to do something to fix how you were feeling?

"This," he said with satisfaction, "is what meditation is all about — learning from what is going on in the moment."

So we can sit with impatience and see where we feel it in our bodies. We can watch an urge rise, a desire come up and we can study it. We can bring our focus and attention to the thought that precedes the feeling. We can feel the desire, observe it moving from place to place in our body. We can listen to our mind scream that we want something now, think we must have it now but actually watch the miracle of the urge going away for a moment. If we do this often enough, that moment between urges will get longer and longer. We will learn from our own experience that we will not die, faint or fall apart if we do not have what we want right away.

This is a significant value of insight meditation.

I have been meditating many years, written books on meditation and led meditation retreats and workshops throughout the country. I feel much better most of the time. But it is important to remember that phrase, "Progress and not perfection," so I don't become too hard on myself when I slip back into the old ways. There is always more to learn. And when we do come to a new place in our recovery, the best way to keep it is to give it away. As it says in *A Course In Miracles,* we teach what we need to learn.

Meditation is a wonderful tool that allows us to learn to quiet our minds. It helps us bring our attention to the moment, to be in the moment and discover that we do not have to run away from the moment, no matter what is going on. Once we have some experience with sitting meditation, we can learn to bring this process to the rest of our day.

Once we learn to quiet our minds, we see what is really going on and learn from our truth. Until we do this, we are reactors locked in the control of people, places and things.

Daily Routine

Once you are out of bed, the basic sitting meditation is a wonderful way to begin your day. I begin my day with spiritual readings and then meditation.

I recommend 20 to 30 minutes of meditation in the morning. Begin with as little as five or ten minutes and build up slowly. The important thing is that you get into a regular routine and do it on a daily basis, no matter what.

The meditation we will do is based on Vispassana Meditation. It is also called Insight Meditation or Mindfulness. It is a very simple meditation that teaches us single-pointed concentration and insight. It helps us to learn awareness and concentration. It is a tool for learning to live in the now, to become aware, and to become insightful during all the hours of the day. It will help us get in touch with a Power greater than ourselves, find peace and serenity and accept, then love ourselves.

Meditation is an important tool for self-knowledge. It enables us to see ourselves as we really are and allows us to let go of our character defects so that we can move on.

Remember that while we are learning to meditate in a sitting position and paying attention to our breathing, we are beginning to learn mindfulness. We will gain insight into our true nature.

Our Own Mind And Body: Our Own Greatest Teachers

We can attend conferences, listen to many teachers, read book after book and still not know anything until we experience it, until we know it with our entire being. We can experience something important and never *know* we are experiencing it, thus not learn from it until we bring awareness to our experiences. Then, when we are in an experience, we *know* it. We *know* it with our senses and with our minds and only then can we learn from it. Only then do we have knowledge.

As we learn to focus on one object, our breath and our minds become trained in concentration. Then we can expand our concentration to different parts of our bodies and our senses. Our senses are like doors that let experiences enter our bodies. We experience with our senses, feel with our bodies, then decide whether the feelings are something we want to keep or push away.

Reacting

Our bodies and our minds are like thermometers. For example, the phone rings and it's the call you've been waiting for. You hear the voice on the other end telling you that you have been selected for the new position you have wanted for so long. Imagine what you would feel at this moment. Excitement! Elation! Maybe even some fear, but if it is a job you have really wanted, mostly happiness. You would share that good news with friends. The feeling would continue and you would want to keep it.

If you heard the voice say you had come in second or that someone else had been chosen for the job, how then would you feel? Dejection. Rejection. Sadness. Depression. Within a few minutes you would be looking for a way to feel better. You might call a friend for some sympathy, eat a candy bar, have a drink or get into bed.

You might go right into denial. Maybe you would tell yourself it didn't matter, you didn't want that job anyway, or if you got it, you probably wouldn't do it well enough, you wouldn't like it eventually or you would be fired, so who cares anyway? The excuses would be made. They didn't like you because you are white or black or red or yellow or too short or too tall. Or a woman. Or a man. Or a homosexual. Or a heterosexual. Or you went to college. Or you didn't go to college. It wasn't your fault.

Our minds find ways to make us feel better, to rationalize and make us feel okay. Our excuses are so solid because they are based on things we can't change about ourselves. They are never about things that are really our responsibility.

Until we learn that we have a choice and that it doesn't have to be always the same, we simply react according to how we feel. We have always done it this way. If we feel good, we want to keep it that way and we want more of whatever it is that makes us feel good. If we feel bad, we don't like it, want to push away or get rid of what we think is the cause. Or we want to find something else to make us feel good again.

So the pattern is that something happens, an event occurs, we perceive it with our senses, our mind judges it as good or bad, pleasant or unpleasant, we feel good or bad according to what our senses tell us and then we . . .

React

Perhaps someone says something sharp to you, yells at you. You hear the words and you feel your entire body tensing, heat begins to cover your body, words rush to your mouth and your hands turn into fists as if they have a mind of their own. You . . .

React

You reach out for a piece of cake and put it into your mouth. Your taste buds respond. It is delicious. Warm sensations fill your mouth and your body. Your mind tells you that it would be okay to have another piece. Your hand reaches out almost as if it has a mind of its own. You are . . .

Reacting

You have been waiting to see a doctor. It took you six weeks to get this appointment. You have been sitting in the waiting room for at least an hour. Babies are crying and the room is warm. You are getting more and more agitated; your impatience begins to take over almost as if your body has a mind of its own. You get up in disgust as you head for the door. You are . . .

Reacting

You are in a relatively good mood. Your spouse walks in the door and asks why there is a toy in the driveway. Before you can begin to answer, you are asked where the cleaning is, and why, how, who, when, etc. You can barely hear anymore as the newer feelings pour over you and take away the good mood that was there just seconds ago.

You are Reacting

Many years ago I was attending a baby shower. There were over 30 people in the room. We all sat in a large circle with the mother-to-be in the center. She thanked each person for their gift. She thanked the woman next to me and then thanked me for mine. I had given her the exact same gift as the person next to me. At a meek attempt at humor I said, "That wasn't very original, was it?" I knew it was a stupid remark. I just knew it was. And I knew that everyone in the room thought it was, too. I was sure they all thought me very foolish. Waves of embarrassment swept over me. I felt ridiculous and vowed I never wanted to feel that way again if I could help it. I vowed I would never say anything in a large group again.

I actually kept that promise for 12 years. It was not until I entered into recovery that I allowed myself to speak before a large group, and only because it was an important part of my recovery program.

I had allowed something that happened one time only to color my next 12 years. I had decided that the future would be the same as the past, and I had not given myself the opportunity for new learning in that area. I had let old feelings rule me and keep me stuck.

Only through acknowledging and opening to suffering can we stop and come to rest, can we find stillness and a deeper ground of goodness and well-being. It is this suffering that prompts us to let go, to live more lightly. By touching this suffering we can awaken the fullest compassion within us . . .

Only when we stop running and accept life with all its dance of change, its ten thousand joys and ten thousand sorrows, with its inherent suffering can we find peace and wisdom.

Jack Kornfield

SUFFERING

So much of our suffering is within our control and most of us do not know it. I *reacted* to my pain and embarrassment, made a decision and didn't know any better until many years later. I was conditioned through ignorance, not stupidity.

The suffering I am speaking of is not the horrible, unnecessary suffering resulting from war, starvation, deprivation or pain. I do not mean the inexcusable suffering caused by the powerful over those who are powerless, the strong over the weak, the rich over the poor or the haves over the have-nots.

When I speak of suffering, I want to make it clear that I mean the suffering that originates from our own conditioning, our own past or our own habitual thinking, consciously and/or unconsciously. Our own ignorance.

I am speaking of a suffering that is so much a part of the human condition that we take it for granted and do not know we can change it. I am speaking of the suffering that we trigger in our own minds and bodies with our own thoughts, memories, perceptions and reactions. I am speaking of a suffering that we can learn to stop as soon as we realize that we have the power to do so.

So much goes on in our subconscious and happens so quickly. A word is said. A feeling is felt. A mood change takes place. All in a split second. Almost simultaneously. As we know, how we think today began in our infancy and developed in our early childhoods. We have learned basic survival techniques that have allowed our lives to be bearable but have distorted our feeling and thinking processes. Therefore when something new occurs, old tapes are turned on and we respond. We are not responding to the actual event of the moment, but rather to old emotions that are stored in our memories, conditioning our responses and going on and affecting new moments in the same old way forever, just as mine was at the shower. I know now that this scene triggered scenes from earlier in my childhood, other embarrassing scenes, such as being laughed at by an uncle when I sang a song at age ten. Or the horrible, sinking feeling I had in high school when I felt less than everyone else to start with or when I was called on to recite and my mind went absolutely blank.

If we have lived with prejudice and have felt the pain of rejection and ostracism, we might well hide the fact that we are Jewish, Polish, lesbian or gay, that our father was a drunk, or that we had been molested as children. Learned secretive, closed behavior can become so much a part of us that we do it automatically. When asked a question as an adult, there might be a slight moment of hesitation while we unconsciously examine whether the question feels safe or threatening. Our early fears of getting hurt again have a spill-over effect into the rest of our lives, keeping us from living in the truth or even seeing the truth for ourselves.

Imagine that your conditioning to life is having a set of colored filters and you are looking out over the ocean. If you hold all of them over your eyes, everything will appear black. If you hold only the yellow filter, it will distort the reality of the color of the blue water and you will see green. If you are holding the red filter, it will distort the reality of the color of the water and you will see purple.

This is exactly how we see reality until we learn to free ourselves of our conditioning. Our reality is that we actually do see green or purple instead of blue. Our eyes do see this color. It registers in our brain. We are telling the truth. But those without filters see true blue. Neither group would be able to convince the others that they are right or wrong about what they are experiencing. Each sees their own truth. It would be wrong to say that people who saw green or purple or any color other than blue were lying to themselves or anyone else. People with filters do not know that the truth they see is not the same as the truth seen by those without filters.

Can we say that there is such a thing as a distorted truth and a real truth? Can we say that one is more truthful than the other? Perhaps we need to take a vote next time we are at the ocean. How many people see green? How many people see purple? Ah, the majority see blue, so that must be the truth.

But wait a moment.

How about at a family gathering?

How about at a family gathering in the living room of a small child? How many people see the father as a kindly man because he has just welcomed you into his home? He has offered you a drink and you are sitting and having a very enjoyable, relaxing and friendly conversation. But how many people see him as a frightening man? Only his young daughter would vote yes to that because before you came in, he had just spanked her and sent her to her room without any supper. Does the majority rule here? Is it up to a vote?

Our minds go through four basic processes over and over again. The trigger to the repetition is our reaction to people, places and things. We continue to suffer if we do not eliminate our reactions and our automatic behaviors.

Awareness of our reactions
is the beginning of the process of change.

Our mood shifts and we do not even know what happened. Our suffering exists because of four processes we repeat over and over again, four automatic actions that are at the root of our suffering.

How Can These Stuck Patterns Be Changed?

With the powerful tool of *noting*, the feelings will pass. *We can achieve this* by simply bringing attention to all the feelings of embarrassment and shame we need to allow those feelings to be just as they are and not judge them and know that we will be all right with feeling foolish for the moment. By not judging, I would have seen that I could have done something foolish and not been foolish. I would have learned that I could have feelings like that and not needed to shut down. The feelings therefore would not have stayed with me stored in my memory, and I would have been free to live the next moment fully alive for the next experience.

Someone says something to us. We hear it with our ears. We receive it into our bodies. We label it. If it is a compliment, we feel pleasant sensations. We feel good, so we like it. We want more. This is the reaction. If we feel upset, we want to stop the words; we want to push them away. We may get angry or defensive. *Reaction!*

If one does not react, it passes away.

Eliminate Past Conditioning

By doing nothing, we eliminate past conditioning. By being an observer, just watching, we see the energy fall away and it does not create new thoughts for new reactions.

Noticing Mindstates

What is the thought that precedes the body getting uptight? We can notice our changing breath to see the condition of our state of mind, a reflection of our mental state. We can see when our breath gets shorter, more shallow or faster. What are the thoughts that are going on? What are the thoughts that precede the reaction? We can pause. We do not have to act. We do not have to react.

We can use *noting* to ease the pain of wanting and desire, and for our addictions, compulsions and obsessions. We can watch our present thoughts and actions and learn what we do that keeps us from being peaceful in the future.

For example we might notice our tension and actually say to ourselves, "Oh, I'm tense," and then look at where we feel it. Where are we holding it? Do we feel it in a rapidly beating heart? Clenched fists? A pain in our throat?

Just notice it and breathe. Breathe in and out from your nose. Bring your attention to the tension and watch it closely. Is it warm or cool? Can you feel it as energy moving in your body? Does it have a size or shape? A color? Does it change as you are noticing it?

The more often you do this, the more you will see that you have a choice. This is the moment of choice, as in the itch that we talked about earlier. As you breathe in and breathe out, you will see this tension change, break up and move. You will see its impermanence. You will see it pass. As long as you watch it without judgment, this will happen. But if you judge what is going on, wanting it to be different and not as it is, the tension will not only stay, but will build and get worse. And your desire for relief will become greater.

If you are aware that you have an addictive personality, you can watch your addictive mind in this struggle and feel a great tension. Watching your mind ask, "Should I? Will I? No! Yes! Do I act out or don't I act out?" you can observe the pain which leads to feeling the need to act out. Here you can . . .

Stop

At this moment of volition. At this moment of choice.

After just a few weeks of meditation, our awareness grows. We are more in tune with the thoughts that precede the feelings. We can bring our attention to these feelings and ask:

"Where do I feel this tension? In what part of my body?"

We can then bring our attention to this tension and pain, and in that moment of pause we can watch it and be okay with it. It can be our full focus without judgment. As we watch it, we can feel it breaking up. As we continue to watch it and breathe in and breathe out, we will feel an easing up of the tension and watch it disappear.

As we begin to feel better without acting out, we can picture ourselves acting out and follow through in our minds with the predictable results. Now that the tension is gone as a result of having made a positive choice not to act out, we find that we do have control.

You are replacing the old, destructive ritual of addiction with a new positive ritual, *noting,* to ease the tension. *Mindfulness . . . noting* is the new positive habit that is now replacing the addictive ritual.

11

BREAKING THE CHAINS OF OUR REACTIONS

The true opposite of depression is not gaiety or absence of pain, but vitality: the freedom to experience spontaneous feelings. It is part of the kaleidoscope of life that these feelings are not only cheerful, "beautiful" and "good," they can display the whole scale of human experience, including envy, jealousy, rage, disgust, greed, despair and mourning. But this freedom cannot be achieved if the childhood roots are cut off.

Alice Miller

As we practice *noting* we will be amazed to see how we can develop our consciousness on a much deeper level of understanding. We can gain amazing knowledge of what makes us tick and how we can be peaceful and healthy.

Watching the thought that leads to a feeling or action can be broken down into four parts:

1. Consciousness
2. Perception
3. Sensation
4. Reaction (1)

Volition lies between the third and fourth part. Here is our moment of choice. Here is our will.

Let's develop this further:

1. Consciousness

The receiving part of the mind receives physical or mental input. Awareness, cognition register occurrences of phenomenon. Also note raw data without assigning labels or making value judgments.

2. Perception

The recognizing factor identifies what has been *noted* by consciousness. Distinguishes, labels, categorizes the incoming raw data. Makes evaluations, positive or negative.

3. Sensation

Input* is received and sensation arises, a signal something is happening. It is either pleasant, unpleasant or neutral.

*If input is not evaluated, input remains neutral. The sensation is the link by which we experience the world with all its phenomena, physical and mental. Whatever arises in the mind is accompanied by a sensation.

Sensation is the crossroad where body and mind meet.

4. Reaction

Once *value* is attached to incoming data, the sensation becomes either pleasant or unpleasant, depending on the evaluation given.

If sensation is pleasant, a wish is formed to prolong and intensify the experience. If unpleasant, the wish is to stop and push it away.

The mind reacts with liking or disliking.

Example:

Someone says something to us. We hear it with our ears. We receive it into our body. We label it. Say it is a compliment. We feel pleasant sensations. We feel good so we like it! We want more! This is the reaction. If it is an insult, we feel upset. We want to stop the words. We want to push them away. We may get angry or defensive. Reaction!

A good example of when I experience this very clearly is when I am in a shopping mall and follow my impulse to go into a bookstore to see if they carry my books. If I go into a bookstore and they have all three, I can feel my energy instantly shoot up. I feel myself beaming, alive and excited. It's a lovely day and all is well with the world.

There might be another bookstore in the same mall. If I should go in there and get a negative response, perhaps they only carry one of my books, or worse none at all and they have never even heard of me, I feel down, dull and negative.

There are a number of lessons here. I can experience all these sensations and know that this is just one of thousands of bookstores and not necessarily indicative of the success or popularity of my books. I can feel myself feel the feelings and move on without a reaction. Or I can take an action step if the response is negative. I can ask to speak to the manager to see if I can get the books into the store.

But if I *react* and let my self-talk run on uncontrolled, I am setting myself up for suffering. I would hold on to these feelings and thoughts and let them control me for the next few hours, taking space in my head and keeping me from being in the present.

If one does not react, the sensation is felt and it passes away!

Now, let's take a look at the Four Processes Of Our Minds again. But this time, let's put a space between steps three and four.

1. Consciousness	= receiving	)	*passive*
2. Perception	= recognize, label, evaluate	)	*passive*
3. Sensation	= pleasant or unpleasant		
	= wish formed	)	*passive*
	SPACE		
4. Reaction	= attraction or repulsion	)	*active*

The crucial link is at the point of sensation. Every sensation gives rise to liking or disliking. These momentary unconscious reactions to liking and disliking are immediatelly multiplied and intensified into *craving, aversion* and *attachment.* This produces misery now and in the future. It becomes a blind habit which we repeat mechanically.

The first three processes, consciousness, perception and sensation, are passive. They just happen automatically. Passivity gives way to attraction or repulsion in the fourth step, that or reaction. This is active and can be stopped. Reaction attracts us toward something we find pleasant. Reaction repulses or backs us away from that which we find unpleasant. The four processes happen so quickly that we are unaware of what is happening. It is only by repeatedly looking at our reactions that we develop awareness at a conscious level. Until we learn to do that, we stay stuck. We are trapped by our past until we break the cycle of automatic thinking, reactions and conditioning.

It is in the *space* between the sensation and the reaction that we can make changes. It is in this *space* that we are at choice. By bringing our awareness to our sensations, we develop serenity and balance. We learn not to react. This gives rise to wisdom. We can learn about our own truth and make choices. We can see that if we do not react, these feelings are impermanent. They arise and then they pass away. By not reacting, we break the chain of suffering. The blind reaction of craving and aversion has stopped.

Back to my bookstore example, I can watch and learn from my reactions. I can see what it feels like to be disappointed and notice where I feel it in my body. I can watch the sensations of jealousy I might feel if other authors are displayed when I am not. I can feel the anger. I can watch all these feelings as they rise and pass away. In my openness and willingness to watch them, the feeling will pass away. But if I react and make a phone call or get upset with the store manager, I am locking in these feelings so they will be stronger the next time I go into a bookstore. My body will be tense, expecting the reaction of pleasure or displeasure.

I obviously cannot control every book buyer for every bookstore. Obviously I cannot even get to every bookstore. I cannot control the shoppers. I cannot control the sales or the buyers' reactions to my books. Once knowing this, I can choose to use my energy in a more positive way.

> *We cannot avoid the truth that life is imperfect, incomplete, unsatisfactory . . . the truth of the existence of suffering.*
>
> *S.N. Goenka*

Eliminate Past Conditioning

> *For the wise have always known that no one can make much of his life until self-searching becomes a regular habit, until he is able to admit and accept what he finds, and until he patiently and persistently tries to correct what is wrong.*
>
> *Bill Wilson*
> *Tenth Step (2)*

By doing nothing, we eliminate past conditioning. By being an observer, just watching, we see the particles fall away and do not create new thoughts for new reactions. Thich Nhat Hanh shows us in his book *The Sun in My Heart* that *we can have an experience, observe the experience and observe the observer observing the experience.* (3)

For example, we can say:

I have an experience that makes me happy.

I am aware that I am happy.

I am aware that I am watching myself be happy.
I am aware that I am aware that I am happy.

In this way we are not reacting to set up new thoughts for new reactions.

We are looking for four truths when looking at suffering:

1. What is it?
2. How does it arise?
3. How does it stop?
4. What is the way leading to cessation?

What is the cause of our suffering, the cause of the cessation of suffering and the path that leads to that cessation? How does all of this help with our addictions, our longings and our cravings?

Jack Kornfield tells us that it is not the object of desire but the energy of the mind that causes suffering. The energy of desire keeps us moving and looking for what is going to do it for us this time and forever. He says that the wanting mind is itself painful, a self-perpetuation habit that does not allow us to be where we are because we are grasping for something else. Even when we get what we want, we want something more or different because the habit of wanting is so strong. (4)

Again . . .

If one does not react, the sensation is felt and it passes away.

Now let's take a look at the Four Processes Of Our Minds again. But this time, let's see some of the things that might be in that space between steps three and four:

1. Consciousness	= receiving	)	*passive*
2. Perception	= recognize, label, evaluate	)	*passive*
3. Sensation	= pleasant or unpleasant		
	= wish formed	)	*passive*

If the sensation is unpleasant we will want to change it. We will have a desire for . . . mood-altering drugs and chemicals, such as alcohol, caffeine, nicotine, cocaine, or tranquilizers or mood-altering actions, such as eating, shopping, gambling, sex or excitement.

If the sensation is pleasant, we will immediately have a fear of losing it and will want to keep it. We will want more of it or we will want to hold on tightly to what we already have.

In this space we can pause and accept the sensation as it is and not react with anything, just be in the moment.

4. Reaction	= attraction or repulsion	)	*active*

Where a wish, volition, will is formed

The crucial link is at the point of sensation. Every sensation gives rise to liking or disliking. These momentary unconscious reactions to liking and disliking are immediately multiplied and intensified into *craving, aversion* and *attachment.* This produces misery now and in the future. It becomes a blind habit which we repeat mechanically.

The first three — consciousness, perception and sensation — are passive. They just happen automatically. Passivity gives way to attraction or repulsion in the fourth step, that of reaction. This is active and can be stopped. Reaction attracts us toward something we find pleasant. Reaction repulses or backs us away from that which we find unpleasant.

By bringing our awareness to this wanting, craving or desire not to feel what we are feeling, we do not have to act out our feeling. We can watch this desire without judgment and, as with the itch, it will go away. This will happen by our noticing the desire without judgment, examining it, bringing our awareness to it and all the sensations that are going on in our body because of the desire. For example, as we notice the feeling, sensation or experience, we can gently say to ourselves, "Oh, a tingling in my arm," "My breath is fast," or "I'm holding my breath."

Personal realization of the truth will automatically change the habit pattern of the mind so that one starts to live according to the truth. Every action becomes directed toward one's own good and the good of others

William Hart (5)

Intention

Joseph Goldstein defines *intention* as the mental factor or mental quality that directly precedes a bodily action or movement. The body moves because of a certain impulse or volition. There is a moment's pause, which he calls "the about-to moment." You know you are about to do something. If you acknowledge the pause and make a note "intending," you will gain deeper insight. Intention is the cause. Movement is the effect. (6)

As we learn to bring our awareness to each moment, we are more and more able to see the thought that precedes the action. As we practice this, we look beneath our actions for the thought, the intention. For example, if we are opening the car door for someone, are we doing this to make them like us? Are we doing this because we want to help them? We might think we are giving advice but are we really trying to bring hurt to someone or show our own superiority?

This parallels the wisdom taught in the Tenth Step. It says that our first objective is the development of self-restraint. We should train ourselves to step back and think, for we can neither think nor act to good purpose until the habit of self-restraint has become automatic. We need to examine our motives carefully in each thought or act that appears to be wrong. Often we see pride, anger, anxiousness, fear. Sometimes rationalization has justified conduct which was really wrong. When we look hard, we can sometimes find a perverse wish to hide a bad motive under a good one.

> *We only transform when we take our suffering consciously and voluntarily; to attempt to evade only puts us into the Karmic cycles that repeat endlessly and produce nothing.*
>
> *Anonymous*

Karma

> *As the cause is, so the effect will be.*
> *As the seed is, so the fruit will be.*
> *As the action is, so the result will be.*
>
> *William Hart*

This is a wonderful example of Karma in Buddhist psychology and another example of how closely related are the thinking of the East and the West. Karma comes from a Sanskrit word which means action. The Buddha used Karma together with volition. Karma is the action. Volition is the motive behind the action.

Most Westerners lack understanding and have preset ideas about the word karma. I would like to ask you to put your concept aside so that you can begin to see in a new light.

When speaking at conferences, there was often a period at the beginning of each talk when I would notice that four or five people would quietly leave the room. While trying not to let this disturb me, I always wondered what I was saying that would cause such strong actions. Finally someone was kind enough to tell me that the word Buddha had turned some people off. They thought that I was speaking about religion, rather than the teachings of a great man. I was sorry that their preset ideas could not allow them to experience the rest of my presentation.

It is a good example of Karma. The intention, the volition not to listen to what they thought would be a religious talk, automatically caused a reaction to leave. Sensations coming from old thoughts and old conditioning created new action in the present but had nothing to do with the truth in the present. I thereafter decided that the Buddha would not mind if I gave him credit later in the talk rather than in the beginning.

In an interview for *Inquiring Mind,* Sharon Salzberg, one of the early founders of the Insight Meditation Society in Barre, Massachusetts, tells us that,

> "The most important element of spiritual life is having a sense of path . . . If we have this, then to actualize it is merely a question of application, time and patience. Without a sense of path, we move from darkness to darkness, not knowing how to get free. An understanding of the law of Karma expresses itself as our sense of path."

She goes on to say that we all want to be happy but we may continually be doing the very things that bring us pain.

According to the laws of Karma, a certain volitional act will bring a certain result.

For example, if you plant an apple seed, you will get an apple tree. No matter how much you pray and beg and plead with the universe, a mango tree will not grow. Karma is the law of connectedness between what we have done and the results for others and ourselves. This is why we have to pay attention to the present and become conscious of our motives. Our present actions bring future results. Our present affects our future. (7)

There are two kinds of Karma:

1. The present Karma.
2. The future Karma.

The present Karma is the quality of mind in which we experience the present. How we experience the present Karma will be how we experience the future Karma. If a sound comes into our consciousness, we hear that sound and have a sensation of pleasantness or unpleasantness. Our perception of the sound will be based on our recognizing the sound.

For example, if the sound is a mail truck outside and we are fearful of receiving a bill that we have not paid (a situation resulting from a past action), we will immediately feel upset and experience many sensations in the present. If we just allow ourselves to feel those feelings without judgment, they will pass and we will stay in the present. But if we resist this upset, want to act out in some way to take away these unpleasant feelings — make a phone call, have a cigarette, candy, whatever — these feelings will continue to be there in the future for us whenever we hear a mail truck.

1. Our past actions produce present feelings.
2. Our reactions to our present feelings create future results.
3. Future results will be experienced as present feelings.

And on and on and on . . . (8)

If we have done something in the past that could result in being arrested, we will feel one set of sensations every time we see a police person. Our past action (Karma) gives us our present feelings.

Once we really begin to look at this and learn to make use of that moment of volition and know that we have a choice, we will take wholesome, moral and healthy actions in accordance with how we want to feel in the present and in the future. When we stop acting in ways that will bring harmful results, we will know we are in charge of our lives.

We understand the law of Karma when we see that our actions bring results. We do not operate in a vacuum. Immediate Karma, the result of our mind, has an immediate effect on how we feel.

We learn that *mindfulness* is the quality of attention which notices without choosing. It is choiceless awareness that, like the sun, shines on all things equally. Mindfulness is breaking the chain of conditioning.

> *When we experience the present feelings, which are a result of past actions, with a mind that is not grasping, not condemning, not forgetting, then we are not creating an action that is producing a new feeling.*
>
> *Joseph Goldstein*

12

WHAT STIRS UP YOUR ENDORPHINS?

Those who seek will see, just as those who eat will be satisfied.

Achaan Chah

The spring of 1990 was a very stressful time for me. The economy in Massachusetts was in great trouble and the housing market had just about come to a standstill. My partner and I wanted to buy a house on Cape Cod, although we still owned a home about 90 miles inland and needed to sell it first. Our goal was to settle down near the ocean and develop a retreat center which we wanted to call Spirithaven. In the meantime we were renting a house on the Cape, while trying to make this all happen.

As it turned out, we could not sell our house or find a new one within our price range. The owners of the one we were renting were returning for the summer and wanted it back. We had only weeks to find another house to rent.

All our affirmations led us finally to rent our own home to a friend on a long-term lease which freed us of any worry about paying our mortgage. However we still needed to find another place to rent until we could find a way to buy a new house. With only days left before we became homeless, we finally found a house suitable to rent for this interim time. It was large enough for us to each have separate space to write yet was within our price range.

Within one week we had to move everything out of the house that we were renting, and then everything out of our own home. The work was exhausting. I felt built-in pressure because I kept changing the deadline of this book. It felt as if I was doing everything but writing it.

Since we wanted to buy a house of our own and the owner wanted to sell we took on a one year lease with an option to cancel after the first six months with only one month's notice. This fact greatly magnified the tediousness of all the moving, sorting, throwing away, repacking and unpacking. We knew it might all have to be done again in six months or soon thereafter. In addition it had been a very cold, sunless winter and spring. I had barely seen the sun and I am emotionally affected by dark days.

I had looked forward to being near the ocean and enjoying the salt air. But most days were too cold to even go near the water, let alone walk on the beach.

One day I was so tired, I felt close to tears. I went out to do some errands and smiled when I saw that the *sun was shining*. I put the top down on my convertible and drove over to a local health food store. I saw a friend who asked how I was and I told her the story of my exhaustion. She said, "You don't look tired. You look terrific!" And I said, "I do? Really?"

I could actually *f e e e l* stress *l e a v e* my body. I could *f e e e l* my body become relaxed and peaceful.

"Thank you!" I said smiling and moved on.

As I continued, I saw a carton on the floor of the store from Health Communications. An order had arrived with six each of all my books, greeting cards and journal. They would soon be on the book shelf to be sold!

I then went over to pick up my cleaning, uneasy because of a disagreement I had had earlier with the clerk. To my surprise the price of $4.00 had been crossed off and the correct price of $2.50 had been written below it. The clerk apologized for the original mistake in the price.

I went back to my car without a tired bone in my body and began to think about what had just occurred in the past 15 minutes that had made such a difference.

What Stirred Up My Endorphins?

Well, first the sun had a positive effect on my mood. Therefore I could put on my Endorphin List:

1. The effect of my surroundings.

Putting my top down was always a freeing, exhilarating experience, especially since I had not had the opportunity for such a long period of time.

2. A positive action step.

"You look terrific!" she said.

3. Seeing new people. Talking with someone who made me feel good.

An order had arrived!

4. Witnessing the results of a previously positive action step.

A woman apologized!

5. The healing power of forgiveness.

I began to examine other changes that made me F E E E L good, changes that were within my power to make for myself.

First we have to free ourselves of the negative blocks that keep us stuck. We have to examine our self-talk and see where we are stuck or burdened. Is our capacity to feel good filled with negativity or have we consciously or unconsciously shut down our capacity to feel?

Feeling All Our Feelings

If we are on any mood-altering substance, we cannot feel all our feelings. Even prescription drugs are given out far too casually. There are some people who need them for varying lengths of time. But if you know truthfully that you are using drugs, pills or alcohol to cover up or change your moods, please take a good hard look at what you are doing.

There was a time in the early '70s, long before my own recovery, when I went to a psychiatrist because I was deeply concerned about my drinking. At that time, I didn't want to stop. I was just *concerned* about my drinking. This psychiatrist knew nothing about alcoholism but was convinced that he could help me. He started me on a long and miserably destructive road that would see me taking 32 different kinds of pills over a two-and-a-half-year period. He treated me as many doctors treat women: with a "There, there, dear! There's nothing wrong with you. Eight visits and a few pills will help." First he wrote a prescription for Librium. When that didn't work, Valium! When that didn't work, he added sleeping pills. At one point I was shaking when I awoke in the morning so he prescribed Artane, an anti-shake pill, but I was shaking from so many pills.

The antidepressants picked me up and the alcohol lifted me even higher before dropping me with a crash. I would then crave more alcohol to feel up again, just to be able to function. Deeply concerned about my extreme mood changes, my ex-husband spoke to my doctor, who, in his lack of understanding about alcoholism did not realize that alcohol is a depressant, which was why I was acting like a yo-yo.

"Aha! She must be a manic depressive. Let's put her on Lithium!" After only a few weeks of this, I remember feeling extremely low, barely feeling at all. It was as if I were walking in deep grayness.

Fortunately, I still had enough soundness of mind to choose to take myself off Lithium. I remember being grateful that there was enough of me left to make that decision.

I made the clear decision to accept the lows that I had always had in my life so that I could feel the highs again.

It is so important that we feel all our feelings. My story is not at all unusual. Pills are still being dispensed far too easily. The favorite drug today is Prozac, for seven million Americans, making it the basis for a seven million dollar industry.

"Have a pill. You'll feel better."

Then we discover that *this* pill damages our kidneys and *that* pill damages our liver.

"Have a joint! It's harmless!" And then we discover it can make us impotent. And there are dangers of birth defects.

Noting is a powerful tool that can help you deal with your feelings, handle your feelings and work through them. It does not require that you ingest anything, but only that you be willing to be with and learn from yourself!

If we don't deal with our feelings today,
they just stick around to give us trouble tomorrow!

FEELINGS AND ENDORPHINS

Imagine you are carrying a bag full of one or more of the following:

- Anger
- Sadness
- Resentment
- Jealousy
- Self-pity
- Fear
- Shame
- Guilt
- Depression
- Confusion

which lead you to feeling . . .

- Dull
- Heavy
- Empty
- Tired
- Disinterested
- Bored
- Depressed

It's time to let them go!

What Stirs Up Your Endorphins?

What Makes You F E E E L . . .

- Good About Yourself ______________________________
- Happy ______________________________
- Creative ______________________________
- Peaceful ______________________________
- Energized ______________________________
- Spiritual ______________________________

Now examine how colors contribute to how you feel.

Red ______________________________

Orange ______________________________

Yellow ____

Green ____

Blue ____

Purple ____

Brown ____

Black ____

White ____

Colors:

If I want to feel good . . .
What colors make me feel good?
What color would I want at work?
What color would I want in my house?

Words:

What words and phrases can I tell myself to stimulate feeling good? ____

Atmosphere:

Do I like bright/soft/dim lights?
Do I like the lights off?
Do I like mood/soft/loud/no music?
Do I like to be alone/with people/in a crowd/with family/with a friend/other . . . ?

Other Things That Affect My Moods . . .

Personal Action Chart For Releasing Endorphins

How would I like to feel now? ____________________

____

What words and phrases can I use to feel this way? ____________________

____

____

____

____

____

____

Affirmations: ____________________

____

____

____

____

____

____

____

Actions:

What action can I take to make me feel this way?
Examples: Do something nice for self/others.
Begin something I have procrastinated about.
Complete something I have left undone.
Organize.
Meditate.
Pray.

Go to a meeting.
Call my sponsor.

Other: ____

____

____

____

____

What colors can I wear to stimulate this feeling? __________

____

____

Other things I can do to contribute to this change: __________

____

____

____

Suggestions

Experiment with the following suggestions to change negative energy into positive energy. Which ones help you? When do you feel this healthy mood change that makes you feel good and can be developed into a positive role in your life?

- Meditate.
- Pick up the phone and talk to someone who cares about you.
- Ask for help from a Higher Power.
- Read spiritual and inspirational literature.
- Go to a 12-Step support group.
- Use the power of words.
- Use the power of prayer.
- Do something good for someone else.
- Write a letter . . . send a card.
- Do *one* thing that you have been putting off. Make a *one-item list.*
- Begin *Noting* when you feel good . . . for example, taking a walk on the beach . . . picking up a good book . . . having a bubble bath . . . so that you can make a positive selection by choice.

- Helping another person is one of the best ways to feel good. Share your strength, hope and experience. Find someone who has had the same experience and share how you came through it. As it says in *A Course in Miracles:* ***We teach what we need to learn.***
- Another choice is simply *being with* the feelings. You will learn that you can handle any feelings. You do not have to escape from them, even in a healthy way. You can have them, experience them and watch them pass so that you will be open for the next moment.
- Do any of the exercises in the back of this book that stir your endorphins and make you F E E E L good.
- Do affirmations as explained further in this book.

We Take Ourselves Everywhere We Go!

I would like to share some of the insights I experienced when I took a wonderful eight-and-a-half-month trip around the country in a 27-foot motor home with my partner in 1989.

I was surprised when I found out that
I took myself along.

The trip was an extraordinary gift to myself, possible only because of my recovery from alcoholism.

We made arrangements to turn over the alcoholism treatment program for women that we created 13 years ago to two very capable women, rented our house for eight months and set out to see our great country.

At the beginning we were both more than exhausted. My partner felt burnt out and I was close to it. We had struggled with our nonprofit company for so long, we needed rest, change and peace. Everything was going to be different. No more business (at least not for a good long time), no more difficulties, no more anyone telling us what to do. We were on our own, doing what we wanted to do, when we wanted to do it. That included getting up when we felt like it, eating when we were hungry, being spontaneous and adventuresome. All in all, just being who we were and having fun.

Suddenly the unexpected hit us with a wallop. My partner Sandy hurt her back and I had to be the driver for three months. We had turned our lives and our will over to the care of our Higher Power on a daily basis. We had turned this trip over to the care of our Higher Power. Suddenly here we were with an unplanned and unpredictable development and fear set in.

I thought, "Is this what it means not to control everything, to be out of control and let it happen? What else will happen that we didn't plan? Is this what it means to *turn it over?*" I found myself under a great deal of tension with the responsibility as sole driver. Not wanting to worry our friends and family back home, we didn't mention it. We were alone with our feelings.

The thought, "What's next?" stayed for a while, but the fear gradually diminished and faith came back as we began to enjoy the wonder and magnificence of this country.

Traveling took much more energy than I had expected. The energy was pouring out, leaving none for creativity. It was exhausting! When driving a motor home, there is so much more to think about than when driving a car. The parking and the turns require much more thought, and backing up requires two people!

Other drivers had no idea that we could not stop as fast as a car and would continually cut in front of us without consideration. It became apparent that no one wanted to be the car behind a motor home. Some people would pass and then get in front and drive slowly. Others would whiz in from the side road with just inches to spare.

We each had contracts for books and the trip was definitely not — at least the way that we were taking it — conducive to writing. I was also putting on workshops and speaking at conferences, so I needed to make all kinds of arrangements for airplane tickets, mail and cleaning. I needed to know exactly where I would be three weeks ahead so I could get my airplane tickets at the lowest rate. I needed to plan to be near a major airport and also had to make arrangements to have my tickets sent to a post office in a town that we would be passing through.

We had waited three years to take this trip. I was torn between the tapes: "There is so much to see and so much to do. This is the only time that I will take a trip like this and I want and deserve this rest and time off" and "I want to take the time to write." I had either been working, going to school or both since the age of 15 and had not taken off more than three weeks at a time since then (even for the birth of my three children).

So wanting to have it all, not wanting to give any of it up, I found myself in conflict. We would try to leave the campground by 10. We usually made it by 11. Then we would travel, sight see and then look for our next place to stay, often pulling in around 8 or 9 PM, definitely too tired to write or work.

I heard my mind battling me with, "I don't have enough time!" "I have too much to do!" and "There is so much to do!"

I often found myself getting caught up in these kinds of thoughts, feeling guilty if I worked because that was taking time from sight seeing and traveling; feeling guilty if I didn't work or write postcards, call my children and do the bills.

I also enjoyed staying in bed until approximately 8 AM because in my working days this had been impossible. However, I did not change the part of my morning routine which included spiritual reading and meditation. This took about an hour.

Suddenly, in one swift, surprising moment of clarity I realized that . . .

I had taken myself along on this trip!

My old thinking had come into this new environment. My self-talk and guilt tapes were shouting at me in the long hours of traveling. Because I was not filling every moment with work or creativity, I had the wonderful gift of hearing the self-talk that was still there when I had nothing to do but just be.

From then on I let it be a learning experience. From then on I used the tools that I had learned, taught and written about to bring peace and understanding, insight and mindfulness. I mustered together everything I read, learned and wrote.

I began to bring attention to the feelings that I was having, discovering their sources. Instead of beating myself for having these unpleasant conflicts, I began to listen to my self-talk.

I found that I was even feeling guilty for not being happy all the time, because who in their right mind wouldn't be 100% happy to be able to be on a trip like this? What expectations I had for myself!

It reminded me of when my mother remarked on neighbors who had two Lincoln Continentals, a beautiful home and a large swimming pool and they were only in their 40s. She said, "What else do they have to look forward to? They are still so young!" She unfortunately was still in the mindset where she thought that if financial needs were met, we would automatically be happy. She dreamed of having a mink stole, a trip to Miami and wall-to-wall carpeting before she died. Her three dreams did come true, yet I believe she still died a very unhappy woman. She just didn't know it could be different.

This is typical thinking from a dysfunctional home: you strive to have all the outside things you want and if you get them, you *should be* happy. And here I was doing the same thing.

So I began to be my own gentle witness, to watch my thoughts and not judge them and to gain insight into my own mind to discover the sources of my dis-ease.

I saw that I had created my own reality.

I realized that I had created my new world just as I had created my old world: a very busy place. Here we were in a 27-foot motor home with an office built in the back, a computer, printer and photocopy machine.

It was I who had made arrangements for putting on workshops and conferences which created a need for me to be in touch with lots of people. I had to write or call concerning all the arrangements. The time difference of two or three hours in different parts of the country made calling even more difficult. Needing to use a pay phone meant often having to wait for other people to finish their calls. Many campgrounds had only one pay phone for everyone's use. Sometimes it meant standing in 100-degree heat, cold drizzle or biting wind and cold.

I also created money issues which I had to deal with. There were times that I waited for checks to come so I could pay my bills, but it might take a week to get to the post office where they were waiting. There was also a great deal of difficulty even getting my mail once I got to the right post office. Often the clerks would say there was no mail for me. I would ask them to look again, and they would come back with the mail.

I found (again) that all I needed to change was my attitude. How many times did I have to learn this lesson before I would *really* learn it?

I had to accept that this is my truth. This is who I am. This is part of my personality.

I actually liked the reality that I had created as long as I wasn't in conflict. I enjoyed getting away and doing the conferences. It was important for me to have this change and make contact with people. I was energized by people contact. It felt good to present my teachings and to share the work I believed in. It was gratifying to witness the changes in people who were practicing the programs I was teaching. And I was certainly grateful to have the income from doing work that I loved and not have to deplete my savings.

At one point, I saw that I had a six-week period during which I would not be doing any conferences and decided not to fill it with any work. I did not want this trip to end without my having the opportunity to experience a long stretch of time of not working more than two or three hours a day. I used this time a few days each week to write. I took two or three hour stretches in the morning, just accepting that as work time.

When traveling, I stayed aware of any thoughts that kept me from peace of mind and that took me away from being in the now. When they did come, which is natural, I practiced noticing them and letting them go. I would let myself feel their effect on my body, feel the full feeling and watch them disappear. If they lingered or kept coming back, I would ask for help to turn them over. If they still stayed and bothered me, I would talk about them.

My partner had been very supportive of my work and my trips to conferences. Part of my conflict came from my own self-talk, such as, "It's not fair for me to be taking time away from our trip and doing this work." She kept assuring me that it was fine but it was not until I heard myself deny what she said over and over that I finally saw it was me doing it to myself again: keeping myself from being happy and in a place of self-pity.

The important difference here was that I began accepting when these thoughts came up. I did not beat myself up for having negative thoughts but just noticed them and came back to my breathing, the same as in sitting meditation.

This experience is an excellent example of how meditation is not just 20 or 30 minutes of sitting, but an important tool to keep with us during our entire 24 hours. We can find what works in our lives that allows us to be free and peaceful, discovering links between the processes of our mind, body and emotions. We can learn how we can be in charge, to be the actor instead of the reactor, and how we can give up the old ways of thinking that keep us bound in misery, guilt and blame.

I have developed some exercises that worked for me on this trip and would like to share them with you. They help me to bring full attention to the moment and to find peace throughout the day.

We can learn to begin and end our day with peace. We can make a choice to move toward feeling centered and at peace in the moments in between. Remember that this is a process. It is progress and not perfection.

13

BECOMING SPIRITUALLY CENTERED

No matter how well we have prepared,
the moment belongs to God.

Sheldon Kopp

There is a very soft moment we experience between sleep and waking. In this moment there are no thoughts. In this moment we truly do experience the moment. We gradually become aware and then . . .

BOOM!

Thoughts begin happening and, depending on the place that we are in emotionally and spiritually, our body begins to respond to our thoughts. It is important to remember that our body does not know the difference between something real or something imagined, and it will react the exact same way in each situation.

So imagine, for example, that you are sleeping in the arms of a loved one. And imagine that your relationship is good, warm and loving. Your thoughts might be of this loving relationship and your first awareness and reaction will be soft and gentle.

Then imagine that you have four interviews this morning, you forgot to set the alarm and you have overslept! You have only 15 minutes to shower and dress. If you take any longer, you will be late for the first appointment.

Everything that you felt was set off by a thought. So how do we begin our day with peaceful feelings?

We begin with that soft warm moment between sleep and waking.

We begin by bringing our attention to the moment and *noting*, not resisting, what is going on in the moment.

How To Start The Day With Guided Imagery

If you like, you can leave your recorder set on the meditation tape (see Appendix II) and just press it on in the morning. Or you can make a tape of your own so that it will be your own voice that you will hear. Or you can remember the essence of the following guided imagery, saying your own words to yourself in the morning. Experiment with all the different ways to find what works best for you. Remember, there are no right or wrong ways to do this, and you cannot meditate wrong. The important thing to remember is that you are willing to be in charge of your life and live in the moment. If you are willing to give up trying to change what is, experience what is without trying to make it better, experience what is without judgment, then wisdom and peace will be yours.

If you are going to be late for an appointment, it still will be better in the long run to take these few minutes for yourself. You will bring a sense of peace and confidence with you, which will be far more effective than rushing in, feeling scattered and being full of excuses and apologies.

You can make or buy a tape (see Appendix II: *Resources* for details) of the following meditations and play them whenever you wish.

To Become Spiritually Centered Before Getting Up In The Morning

As you become aware that you are awake, gently notice whatever thoughts are going through your mind.

Gently notice your reactions to your thoughts.

Be with your reactions.

Be with all the feelings that are taking place right now.

What were the thoughts that preceded the feelings?

Let everything be just as it is and notice the feelings pass by.
Gently bring your attention to your breathing.
Breathe in deeply through your nose
and gently say to yourself:
Good morning, (add your name)!
Breathe in deeply through your nose.
Know that every time you breathe in, you are freeing more and more endorphins to flow through your body.
Every time you breathe in, you release all your endorphins to flow through your body,
Energizing, soothing and healing you . . .
Feeling your breath entering your nose.
Follow as it goes completely into your body.
Filling your chest . . .
Flowing through your shoulders . . .
Feel it flowing through your arms and your wrists, your hands and your fingers . . .
Feel it flowing down your back and into the small of your back, down into your hips and your legs and into your feet.
F E E L the *energy* of your *endorphins!*
Know that you are *now* being filled with positive, loving, healing energy.
You are *now* being filled with loving energy.
You are *now* connecting with all the healing powers of the universe!
You are *now* being nurtured and loved.
You are *now* at peace.

Peace At Any Time . . . To Become Spiritually Centered Anytime And Anywhere

When we are in a peaceful mood, we are usually not aware of it. We feel content and go about our life. Awareness comes when we compare our peace with another feeling.

For example, if someone has just insulted me and I still feel all right, my ego-centered thoughts might go something like: "My, haven't I grown! Usually a comment like that would make me angry, depressed or defensive. It feels good not to be that way today!" I feel peace by comparison with nonpeaceful feelings. As I continue to grow and my acceptance of the moment is more usual for me, I will be far more aware of the times that I do *not* feel peaceful. It is to times like these that this portion of the tape is directed.

When you become aware that you are agitated, upset, unhappy or experiencing any feeling that is taking you away from peace, gently notice whatever thoughts are going through your mind.

Can you remember the thought that preceded the feeling?

What was the thought that came before the upset?

Be with the feeling! Don't resist it. Don't wish it to be different than what it is. Accept it just as it is and be as gentle as you can with yourself. Don't judge it as good or bad.

Bring your attention to your breathing.

Notice how it has changed from regular and peaceful to either short or shallow. Maybe you're hardly breathing at all. Maybe you are holding your breath so that there is no breath to feel at all.

Know that any change in your breath is a change in your endorphin flow. Know that stress and anxiety block your endorphins. Know that when your endorphins are blocked, you lose your sense of well-being.

Remember that *you* are in charge of this moment.

Remember that *you* do not have to be a reactor.

Know that you have all the *P O W E R* you need to let this feeling be just what it is: a feeling.

Know that you are not the feeling.

Know that this feeling will pass and that you will again feel peaceful through any circumstances.

Let yourself be aware of all that is going on in your mind and your body.

Let yourself be aware of all your feelings and where they are stored in your body.

F E E E L the feelings.

Let yourself *F E E E L* the feelings.

Release any resistance you might have to feel your feelings.

Watch how they change and begin to move away as you let yourself feel them.

As you let yourself accept them, breathe in deeply through your nose and gently say to yourself, *Hello* (your name)!

Breathe in deeply through your nose

Feel your breath entering your nose.

Follow it as it goes completely into your body,

Filling your chest . . .

Flowing through your shoulders . . .

Feel it flowing through your arms and your wrists, your hands and your fingers. Feel it flowing down your back and into the small of your back, down into your hips and your legs and into your feet.

Know that you are *now* being filled with positive, loving, healing energy.

You are *now* being filled with loving energy.

You are *now* being nurtured and loved.

You are *now* at peace.

Noting Our Feelings Without Judgment

Here is an exercise to help you bring your attention to your thoughts and learn how they affect your feelings. This exercise can also be used to center yourself and to bring you peace.

Sit quietly for a few minutes and bring your attention to your breathing.

Just be with your breath as you breathe in and out from your nose.

Be aware of the space that you are in.

Bring your attention to the places where there is physical contact, places where your body touches the floor, the rug or the chair. Notice where your hands touch your body. Be aware whether your hands are warm or cool. Are they tense or relaxed?

Place your right hand over your left hand. Bring your attention to the bottom of your right thumb. Be aware of your right hand over your left knuckles. Be aware of the palm of your left hand.

Imagine that there is a circle of light surrounding you and know that you are safe in that circle.

Now be aware of any clothing that you feel against your body. Be aware of any texture or weight that you can notice.

Let yourself imagine a time when you were embarrassed in front of other people. How does that feel in your body?

Do you notice any changes of breath?

Any changes of temperature?

Know that you are all right, you are only reliving a memory and it cannot affect you today. Allow yourself to feel these feelings without judgment. Let them be just as they are.

What is happening with your feelings?

Just notice what they do . . . where they go.

Now let yourself remember a time when you felt terrific! A time you set out to do something and did it. What are the feelings that come to you with this memory? In what parts of your body have you stored these feelings.

Do you notice any changes of breath?

Any changes of temperature?

Know that you are all right; you are only reliving a memory. Know it cannot affect you today. Allow yourself to feel these feelings without judgment. Let them be just as they are.

You can do this exercise with any feelings or memories of any feelings. Just let yourself experience the feelings, *noting* them without judgment. Then let them go. When you are ready to let them go . . .

Be aware of your right hand over your left hand.

Be aware of any temperature that you feel.

And then bring your attention back to your breathing.

Always be very gentle and non-judgmental with yourself.

Be with your breath for a few minutes and then come back to your room. Just be sure that you count to five before your open your eyes.

PART THREE

Let yourself be silently drawn by the stronger pull of what you really love.

Rumi

14

The Healing Power Of Meditation

The breath is the link between the body and the mind.

The Buddha

Over 2500 years ago the Buddha passed down the message that meditation was the answer to healing.

There is now scientific proof that meditation *is* healing.

Dr. Bernie Siegal says that people who meditate, as well as those who confide traumatic experiences to diaries rather than repressing them, have an enhanced immune function. (1)

Dr. Herbert Benson was one of the first people who scientifically documented the effects of meditation on the body. He documented states of profound rest in humans who practiced Transcendental Meditation (TM). He proved that this state could be elicited through any form of mental concentration that distracted the individual from the usual concerns of the mind. He called this innate, hypothalamic mechanism the *Relaxation Response.* He theorizes that when we engage in right-hemisphere brain activity, we may raise the level of serotonin, the neurotransmitter associated with a sense of calmness and pain relief. Stressful gloom-and-doom thinking activates our left brain and may produce a depletion of norepinephrine and dopamine which are implicated in depression and other disorders. (2)

Benson describes the effects of his form of meditation which he calls the *Relaxation Response:*

- Heart rate and blood pressure drop.
- Breathing rate and oxygen consumption decline (because of the profound decrease in the need for energy).
- Brain waves shift from an alert beta-rhythm to a relaxed alpha-rhythm.
- Blood flow to the muscles decrease and instead, blood is sent to the brain and skin, producing a feeling of warmth and rested mental alertness.

Joan Borysenko wrote in her book *Minding The Body, Mending The Mind* that it was by learning to induce the relaxation response that she began to reverse symptoms that were severe enough to send her to the emergency room. (3)

Many people I've worked with have had improvements with physical conditions when they have meditated. One woman, for example, no longer needed insulin shots for her diabetes. Three different women had their menstrual cycles begin after not having them for two, five and ten years, respectively.

I have not worked in depth with people with serious illnesses as my field is mainly addiction, co-dependency and adult children of alcoholics. In this population, many have experienced wonderful results from meditation. Co-dependency issues, emotions, job-related problems, relationships and finances have all been positively affected. Back, sleep and eating problems have improved. But the most profound results are related to addiction and dependencies.

People have got off pills, including tranquilizers, sleeping pills and anti-depressants. They have got off alcohol and drugs. It is one thing to get off something and it is another to stay off. The most profound result is that . . .

Among the people I've worked with, no one who meditates on a daily basis has picked up a drink or a drug.

The emotional environment we create within our bodies can activate mechanisms for destruction or repair. (4) Siegal believes we have the ability to train our bodies to heal and eliminate illness. Through meditation and altering our lifestyles, we can gain access to the superintelligence within us. This superintelligence is the message carried by psyche and soma via the peptides — the printout of our DNA, the code of life itself. It makes us who we are and if we listen, it will keep us on our path. (5)

Guided Imagery

One difference between meditation and imagery is that meditation is passive and imagery is active. Imagery is when we or someone else guides our imagination. When we do guided imagery, powerful results can happen.

One theory is that when we engage in right hemisphere brain activity, we may raise the level of serotonin, the neurotransmitter associated with a sense of calmness and pain relief. Stressful gloom-and-doom thinking activates our left brain and may produce depletion of norepinephrine and dopamine, which are implicated in depression and other disorders. The theory is that by engaging in positive imagery, we may encourage self-healing processes by elevating serotonin while protecting the left hemisphere from catacholamine depletion. (6)

Meditation and imagery are right brain activities.

Right And Left Brain Pictures

Left Brain	**Right Brain**
Analytical	Intuitive
Logic	Creative
Language	Artistic
Thinking	Images
Words	Feelings
Processes information sequentially	Processes information simultaneously
	Grasps large contexts of events

In their Nobel prize-winning work, Roger W. Sperry, Ph.D., and his collaborators at the University of Chicago and later at the California Institute of Technology, found that in a real sense we have two brains and that they are simultaneously capable of independent thought. The right-brain point of view may reveal the opportunity hidden in what seems to be a problem. The imagery it produces often lets you see the big picture.

Benson suggests that we have an inner conflict when we want to change. The left side of the brain tells us we can't change while the right says we can. He has had positive results when patients have elicited the Relaxation Response through meditation, prayer or other techniques. They can set the stage for important mind-and-habit-altering brain change. Scientific research has shown that electrical activity between the left and right sides of the brain become coordinated during certain kinds of meditation and prayer. (7)

Research has shown that when we mentally picture our bodies doing something, physical changes can occur, such as muscle expansion, increased blood pressure, altered brain waves and sweat glands. We can also increase our body temperature with "hot thought," such as scenes at the beach or desert. We increase our blood flow and the warmth of our hands and other parts of the body.

Fantasy, which is a form of imagery can create dopamine, serotonin and endorphins. (8)

Martin M. Rossman, M.D., writes that imagery has been shown to affect:

Heart rate.
Blood pressure.
Respiratory patterns.
Oxygen consumption.
Carbon dioxide elimination.
Brain waves rhythms and patterns.
Electrical characteristics of the skin.
Local blood flow and temperature.
Gastrointestinal motility and secretions.
Sexual arousal.
Levels of various hormones and neurotransmitters in the blood.
Immune system function. (9)

> *Sought through prayer and meditation to improve our conscious contact with God* as we understood God, *praying only for God's will for us and the power to carry that out.*
>
> *Step 11*
> *12 Steps And 12 Traditions*
> *(10)*

Bringing Meditation Into Our Everyday Life

Now that we have seen the medical and scientific power of meditation, what is meditation and how can we do it? There are so many different kinds, so many different definitions.

I will share with you the kind of meditation that I personally do and teach. My life has changed dramatically because of it and I have seen many other people become transformed and healed, too.

I began my recovery from alcoholism in 1973. Meditation was suggested as a step in recovery. I had absolutely no idea what it was all about until I had an opportunity to learn about Transcendental Meditation in 1978. Transcendental Meditation, or TM as it is more popularly known, is a form of meditation where one repeats a mantra over and over again. A mantra is a word or phrase that is personally given to you by a master or teacher.

In 1978 a TM teacher came to Serenity House, the halfway house for women which is a part of the alcoholism rehabilitation program for women that I co-founded and was co-directing with Sandy Bierig. This teacher, Bob Ferguson, wished to teach the staff TM so we could pass it along to the residents.

He said that those with low self-esteem will not meditate. That statement said two things to me. One, that I wouldn't meditate because I knew I had low self-esteem; and two, because I knew I had low self-esteem, I didn't want to continue to feel that way. The first one worked as a challenge. If someone says I can't do something I want to do, it's usually enough to make me want to prove them wrong. I have meditated every day since, not missing once. I pass on the same challenge to all of you. I have already written about this in my first book, *The Journey Within: A Spiritual Path to Recovery.* (11) But I just couldn't miss this opportunity to challenge all you new readers!

I found TM very calming and helpful. It helped me begin to develop an inner discipline that had been lacking in my life. Each morning I took time for inspirational reading and 20 minutes of TM.

After five years of practicing Transcendental Meditation, I had a strong sense that there was "more." What that "more" was, I did not know.

When I discovered Vipassana Meditation in 1984, I knew.

What excited me most about Vipassana Meditation was that it was so compatible with the 12 Steps of recovery. First published in 1953, the *Big Book* explains the process undergone by the earliest founders of Alcoholics Anonymous.

The word *Buddha* means *to be awake.* The story goes that the Buddha sat under the bodhi tree and meditated for 40 days and 40 nights to try to find a way to end world suffering. At the end of this time he rose and shared his truth with the first person he met. He said, *"I am awake."* He meant that he was awake in the moment. He was not in his past. He was not in his future. He was fully alive and awake in the moment, in the *now.* He fully accepted what was. He didn't long for what he didn't have. He didn't push away what he did have. He was at peace with life in the moment.

The root-word *Buddha* means to wake up, to know, to understand. He or she who wakes up and understands is called a Buddha, and the capacity to wake up, to love and to understand is called Buddha nature. (12)

In the *Twelve Steps and Twelve Traditions,* Bill Wilson tells us that as a result of following the path laid out by the founders of AA, we too will have a Spiritual Awakening. (13)

Insight Meditation

Since the time of the Buddha, teachers have been guiding people in Vipassana Meditation, also called Insight Meditation or Mindfulness. It is only recently, within the last 15 years or so, that Vipassana has been gaining popularity in the Western Hemisphere. Sitting groups in retreat centers, temples and universities have sprung up all over the country.

Vipassana means introspection or insight that totally purifies the mind. Specifically, this is insight into the impermanent nature of the mind and body. *Vipassana-bhavana* is the systematic development of insight through the meditation technique of observing the reality of oneself by observing sensations within the body.

Bill Wilson writes that every time we are disturbed, no matter what the cause, there is something wrong with us.

> For the wise have always known that no one can make much of his life until self-searching becomes a regular habit, until he is able to admit and accept what he finds, and until he patiently and persistently tries to correct what is wrong. (14)

He goes on to teach that . . .

> Our first objective will be the development of self-restraint . . . We should train ourselves to step back and think . . . for we can neither think nor act to good purpose until the habit of self-restraint has become automatic . . . We need to carefully examine our motives in each thought or act that appears to be wrong. Often we see pride, anger, anxiousness, fear. Sometimes rationalization has justified conduct which was really wrong. A perverse wish to hide a bad motive under a good one." (15)

The 12 Steps Of Recovery

1. Admitted we were powerless over alcohol (here you can substitute the word alcohol with drugs, gambling, emotions, food, other people, etc.) and that our lives had become unmanageable.
2. Came to believe that a power greater than ourselves could restore us to sanity.
3. Made a decision to turn our will and our lives over to the care of God as we understood God.
4. Made a searching and fearless moral inventory of ourselves.
5. Admitted to God, to ourselves and to another human being the exact nature of our wrongs.
6. Were entirely ready to have God remove all these defects of character.
7. Humbly asked God to remove our shortcomings.
8. Made a list of all persons we had harmed and became willing to make amends to them all.

9. Made amends to such people whenever possible, except when to do so would injure them or others.
10. Continued to take personal inventory and when we were wrong, promptly admitted it.
11. Sought through prayer and meditation to improve our conscious contact with God *as we understood God,* praying only for God's will for us and the power to carry that out.
12. Having had a spiritual awakening as a result of these 12 Steps, we tried to carry this message to alcoholics (replace with word of your choice here) and to practice these principles in all our affairs.

(RF) (16)

In the first steps, we learn that we are powerless, that our lives have become unmanageable. We turn our lives and our will over to a power greater than ourselves. Now begins a lifetime process of self-examination. The following steps teach how the character defects or weaknesses that we discover through self-searching must be shared with a power greater than ourself and another human being. Then these flaws must be turned over, let go of to a Higher Power so that we may go on with our lives.

Next we made an examination of the harms done to self and others, made direct amends whenever possible but only when the amends would not hurt self or others. We continued to take daily inventory and when wrong, promptly admitted it. And we sought through prayer and meditation to improve our conscious contact with God as we understand God, seeking only for knowledge of God's will for us and the power to carry it through. Action is the key word in Step 12 so that we may readily give all the help that we have received to those still suffering. (17)

Insight meditation gave me the tools to do step 11. It gave me new tools to do a deeper fourth step, a deeper third step and seventh step and all the steps in between. It teaches one to accept what is without struggling to change it. It is the struggling to change that brings us suffering.

> . . . We can break through the conditioned patterns of the mind and come to know the deepest truth for ourselves. *That which was hidden becomes seen,* that which was overturned becomes upright. We can live our lives in harmony, with a greatness of heart, a clear mind and come to know peace.
>
> Joseph Goldstein (18)

15

Personal Tools

Cultivate your own guru, which is awareness,
the best friend who will not deceive anyone,
then you will learn to understand yourself,
and you will not go in a false direction.

Dhiravamsa

I designed a simple program that I presented in *The Journey Within: A Spiritual Path To Recovery* combining meditations, visualizations and affirmations. In my second book, *Learning To Live In The Now,* I broke this program down into six sections, following the six-week course that I teach. It can either be done a week at a time or at whatever pace you need to set to complete each section. This program is called *Meditation Plus* and presents a basic Spiritual Prescription for growth and change. It consists of the following seven steps:

1. ***Meditation*** which clears and quiets our minds and leads to . . .

2. ***Awareness And Insight.*** We begin to see what is between ourselves and God. We begin to shine a light on our stumbling blocks. We can then listen with clarity to God's will for us.
3. ***Finding Peace In Our Inner Sanctuary.*** We learn how to go within to find our own peace, our own truth.
4. ***Acceptance.*** We begin to forgive and accept ourselves so we can become free from yesterday and tomorrow.
5. ***Empty Ourselves.*** We empty ourselves from all that is keeping us from our highest good, our highest purpose. We become empty so that we can refill.
6. ***Visualizations*** and
7. ***Affirmations.*** We use visualizations and affirmations to gently soften our journey to positive change and help us to create a new positive self-image.

On the following pages you will be able to experience all of these and learn how to incorporate them into your full everyday life. You will learn the very basic meditation that you can use at all times.

You will learn that you cannot meditate wrong!

You will have the transformational opportunity to recycle your pain into gifts, your past into presents.

- You will discover the path to connect with your Inner Goddess, your Spiritual Guide.
- You will learn that your feelings and thoughts are okay.
- It is a safe and healthy way to transform your secrets and shame.
- You will learn skills to center you and bring you peace throughout your continued journey in recovery.
- You will find what has been blocking you from being the very best that you are.
- And you will discover your own special gifts that have been long buried deep within you.

16

Basic Sitting Meditation Instructions (1)

Sought through prayer and meditation to improve our conscious contact with God as we understood God, praying only for God's will for us and the power to carry that out.

Step 11 (2)

Before actually going into the basic meditation, let's take some time to talk about meditation and the how's and where's of it.

What Is Meditation?

In part meditation is an exercise. It is an exercise we practice over and over again. From this practice we learn many things. It teaches us single-pointed concentration which is about focusing on one primary object, such as the breath, so that all other things become secondary.

Meditation is the quieting of our minds. As we concentrate on one primary object, the voices that continually go on in our minds become quieter and quieter, less and less powerful and controlling.

Many people live their entire lives not even knowing that the voices that go on in their heads can be stopped, or at least quieted down and stopped for a while. They live their lives reacting to all thoughts and impulses, never knowing that they can be in charge of their lives and can choose their thoughts and their actions.

Meditation is a tool that can bring us to a place within where we can just notice these thoughts and go back to our primary object of concentration.

Meditation is the bridge between your outside world and your inside world.

Meditation teaches us the Spirit/Mind/Body connection.

Bill Wilson tells us that prayer is asking while meditation is listening. (2) We have to be quiet before we can hear.

An excellent definition has been printed on a brochure of the Insight Meditation Society (IMS) in Barre, Massachusetts:

> Insight Meditation . . . Vipassana . . . is a simple and direct practice . . . the moment to moment investigation of the mind-body process through calm and focused awareness. Learning to experience from a place of stillness enables one to relate to life with less fear and clinging. Seeing life as a constantly changing process, one begins to accept pleasure and pain, fear and joy and all aspects of life with increasing equanimity and balance. As insight deepens, wisdom and compassion arise. Insight meditation is a way of seeing clearly the totality of one's being and experience. Growth in clarity brings about penetrating insight into the nature of who we are and increased peace in our daily lives.
>
> As we quiet our minds we are able to develop equanimity.
>
> Equanimity is the quality of mind and heart that, when developed, allows one to meet every kind of experience with both strength and a softness or fluidity that doesn't get caught up by circumstances. To discover its power within is one of the greatest joys of practice. (3)

Meditation makes it possible for us to quiet down so that we can see. It is the light on our path to change.

How To Dress

Wear comfortable, loose clothing. Be sure it is appropriate for the weather. It is best to dress so that you will not be conscious of warmth or cold.

How To Sit

Sit with your back as straight as possible and with your chin tucked down slightly so that the back of your neck is straight. If you can, sit yoga style with your legs crossed. In a lotus or semi-lotus position, you will have the best balance for longer periods of sitting. At first this may seem very uncomfortable and your body might not want to sit that way. You may wish to get a book of yoga exercises and learn how to stretch your body so it can be comfortable in that position. The more you try it, the easier it will get.

If you cannot learn the lotus or the semi-lotus, you can sit crossed-legged, Indian style.

If you are sitting on the floor, it can be very helpful to sit with your buttocks on a small pillow with your legs on the floor. This is good for balance. If you find that you cannot manage this position, you can sit in a chair with your feet on the floor. Be sure your back and your neck are straight and your chin is slightly up.

Where To Meditate

I suggest that you pick a regular place for meditating if this is possible in your lifestyle. Find a peaceful place, a place that makes you feel good. You could put a plant, picture or favorite saying in your meditation area. In other words, make it your special place. Then just walking by will give you a feeling of peace. It will be a place that makes you smile.

You can also meditate outside, at the beach, in the woods or in your own backyard.

Meditating with a group is very powerful. You can do this while taking meditation lessons or find a support group. Or start your own. In a center the environment is usually more controlled. Noises are at a minimum and space is comfortable. This is a good way to learn and a good way to practice, but it is important to realize that this controlled environment cannot always to be duplicated at home. If you expect it, disappointments will occur. As there is often more power when meditating with a group, it can be a very meaningful experience.

Retreats are wonderful places to get away and deepen your meditation experience. Again, remember that these are in ideal conditions and when you return home, reality will set in and you will have to adjust.

How Long?

It is suggested that you begin with 20 minutes in the morning and 20 minutes in the evening or late afternoon. If this is difficult and you can only do it once a day, make this time in the morning. This will begin your day with good energy. If 20 minutes seems too long, do less. Even five minutes is a beginning and better than nothing at all.

It is also helpful to meditate at the same time everyday. Find a time for yourself when it is most quiet. Ask that this time be respected by all and that you are not interrupted.

At times of stress or sickness, you can meditate more often. A mini-meditation is wonderful. In the midst of stress at home or in the office, excuse yourself for a few minutes and sit by yourself and meditate. It can be as refreshing and tranquilizing as a full night's sleep.

Why Breathe Through The Nose And Not The Mouth?

It is a discipline. We eat with our mouth. We breathe with our nose. It is clear and balanced. You do not have to make the decision of nose or mouth.

What If I Think A Lot?

It is absolutely normal to have thoughts. Just notice them and go back to your breathing. You will learn to notice your thoughts and come back to your breathing. By experiencing them, watching them as if you were an observer, your thoughts will just be there and then go away. If you notice yourself planning for something in the future, just notice it and go back to your breathing. If you notice that you are letting in a past memory, just notice that and return to your breathing.

Through this process of watching your thoughts, you will quickly see that you always have thoughts, whether meditating or not. This is a valuable lesson in learning to concentrate wherever you are. You will see how often your thoughts take you away from the present, whether in a conversation with someone, while reading a book or attending a lecture. You will begin to see that you are very often not where you think you are! As you learn to come back to your breathing while in your sitting meditation, you will also be learning how to come back to your conversation, your book or your lecture.

While practicing your meditation, just notice your thoughts and come back to your breathing. Don't resist them or struggle with them. And above all, do not judge or put yourself down for having thoughts. Just notice them, make a mental note of them and go back to your breathing.

Must The Meditation Place be Completely Quiet?

There will always be noise. There is a wonderful story a meditation teacher told about this. He had planned for a long time to take a day off and go to the woods all alone to meditate. He packed a backpack with his favorite lunch, his favorite book and off he went.

The weather was perfect. He walked deep into the woods and found a wonderful spot with a tree he could lean against. He took his backpack off, settled in comfortably and began to meditate.

Within minutes, squirrels began to quarrel above him. Acorns and leaves began to fall. Birds became disturbed and began to chirp.

He struggled with thoughts of leaving. He struggled with disappointment and irritation. After several moments of upset, he simply smiled and went back to his breathing. He noticed the noise and went back to his breathing. Soon the noise of the squirrels and the acorns and the birds became part of the moment, part of his meditation. By accepting the noise as a normal part of a day in the woods, and that he was powerless over the noise, it no longer had any power to upset him. He became peaceful in the moment.

As with thoughts, just notice the noises and go back to your breathing. Don't try to block them out. Don't resist them. Just hear them and bring your attention back to your breathing.

Impulse Control

An important additional value of meditation is that it is a wonderful tool to show us that we can be in charge of our lives. It teaches us impulse control. We can learn wonderful lessons from our body and how we respond to its demands. We don't always have to fix things or make them better.

For example, if a foot should fall asleep, you do not have to move. You can just be with the experience and see what it feels like, feeling all the sensations of a sleeping foot. If your body says it wants to move, you can just be with that sensation, watching it, feeling the feelings of wanting to move and yet not moving. If you decide you want to come out of meditation early, just notice how you react to that wish. You can stay in meditation and watch yourself want to leave. *You* are in charge. Not the mind that says, "Let's quit!"

If you have an itch . . . don't scratch! It is very exciting to know that you do not have to scratch an itch. It takes a moment for the itch to send a message to your brain which sends another message to your hand to scratch. In that moment, by bringing your attention to the itch instead, the itch will go away. This is an important lesson in impulse control.

The Difference Between Meditation, Guided Imagery And Visualizations

Before we begin to meditate, it is extremely important for you to understand the difference between meditation and guided imagery or visualization.

Meditation

Meditation is a quieting down of our thoughts so that we can be present in the moment and gain insight into exactly what is going. *Meditation is being present and aware of the moment.* The practice of meditation brings us to a place of quiet where we may hear our Higher Power and know our own truth. As it tells us in the 11th step, this is where we can improve our conscious contact with God.

Meditation is passive. Meditation is not active. Meditation is in the *now.* We do not direct our thoughts. We accept whatever comes up in our minds or bodies or feelings. We let meditation happen . . . experiencing the results of what is.

We have no expectations when we meditate. We do not meditate specifically for peace, quiet or stress reduction, although we often do feel all of this as a result of meditation. Ideally we meditate and accept exactly what we get in the present moment.

Guided Imagery And/Or Visualization

The phrase *guided imagery* and the word *visualization* are really the same and are often used interchangeably. We guide ourselves or someone guides us to change what we see, think, smell, touch, taste, feel and imagine in our minds and our bodies.

We guide our minds and senses for a specific purpose. We visualize ourselves in another time, another place, another mood. We go to somewhere other than the reality of the present moment. We do this on our own or we listen to a guide who is present or on tape — someone who directs our imagination to be somewhere else other than the present moment.

We make something happen, experiencing what we chose to experience in the time setting in which we chose to be.

Both *are* active and directed.

In guided imagery or visualizations we are *doing*. In meditation we are *being*. Sometimes it is necessary just *to be*.

Guided Imageries Or Visualizations Do Not Take The Place Of Meditation

We meditate on a regular basis. We make a commitment to improve our conscious contact with our Higher Power for a specific period of time each day. Once having fulfilled this disciplined commitment and while in a place of stillness we can add other experiences to our sitting if we so choose.

Meditation helps you discover who you are and what is going on for you in the present moment.

Know that you are perfect, just the way you are in this moment. Everything you have done in your entire life has brought you to this moment. All that you have gone through has given you the strength to be here right now. Celebrate yourself right now for all that you are.

Any time that you do not believe this, just give it lip service, *act as if it is true* until you feel it.

Guided Imageries and Visualizations are wonderful tools to help us rehearse our feelings and to rewrite our negative tapes into positive healthy ones.

Our thoughts are the beginning of all our feelings and we can choose how we feel at all times. This takes practice. So begin your practice now.

Coming Out Of Meditation Gently

If at any time you wish to come out of meditation, just stop and count to five before you open your eyes. The reason for this is that when you meditate, you are in a deeper state of consciousness. We go from a beta state, our regular awake state, into an alpha state, in meditation. By counting to five before you open your eyes, you will come up gently and slowly and then be able to resume your life in beta state without any negative effects.

If the telephone should ring or you have any other disturbances that take you out of meditation sharply, just return to your meditation as soon as you can for five more minutes. Then slowly come out . . . counting to five before you open your eyes.

Stay as long as you wish in any place that you are in, regardless of how much time seems to be passing.

I would also suggest that you have a notebook and pen next to you so that you record feelings and insights when you return to your beta state.

If you begin to leave any guided meditation, just notice the thoughts that have taken you away. Very gently, without judgment, come back to your breathing. If at any time you feel yourself leaving, it is helpful to ground yourself by feeling the connecting points where your feet touch the floor, your hands touch your body or your clothing touches your skin. Notice those points of connectedness and come back to your breathing.

Sometimes fear takes us away. We don't want to look. We don't want to change. Just know that whatever comes up is for your higher good. If it is negative or destructive, it is time to see that, feel it and release it. Know that whatever it is that you don't want to see is holding you back. Freedom is on your path . . . one step at a time.

17

BASIC MEDITATIONS

Wholeness exists to the extent the individual is conscious of and receptive to her or his innermost self. The more aware and accepting a person becomes of her or his inner images and motivations, the more she or he becomes healed.

Marsha Sinetar

Begin by getting yourself in a comfortable position and make sure that your clothing is loose and not binding. You can sit upon a cushion with your legs crossed Indian style on the floor or you can sit in a chair with your feet flat on the floor. Please do not lie down as that is too conducive for sleeping. Sit with your back as straight as possible and your chin tucked down slightly so that the back of your neck is straight. In this way energy can flow through your body without being blocked. If you wear glasses, you might find it comfortable to remove them.

Now I will begin by guiding you in a gentle meditation to help you relax and let A L L your stress and anxiety leave your mind and your body.

Pause as long as you like at any point in this guided meditation.

Now . . . close your eyes very . . . very . . . gently.

And spend a few minutes

Bringing your F U L L attention to your breath . . .

As it goes in and out from your nose.

Just be with your breath as it goes in and out from your nose . . .

Now bring your F U L L attention to the top of your head and feel relaxation flowing A L L over your scalp . . .

Then relax your forehead . . .

And bring relaxation to the muscles around your eyes

And your eyelids.

Feel relaxation flowing over all the bones and muscles of your face . . .

Especially along your jaw which is a common place to hold tension.

Now get in touch with the softness of your mouth as it is closed very very gently.

Relax your throat . . .

And let all your stress . . . all your tension . . .

Pour down the back of your neck . . . down through your shoulders . . .

Down through your arms . . . wrists . . . hands . . .

Feel all your stress . . . resistance . . . all your tension and anxiety . . .

Pouring into your fingers . . .

And then leaving your body through the tips of your fingers.

Completely leaving your body through the tips of your fingers.

And now bring relaxation to your chest . . .

Down through your diaphragm . . .

Relaxation flowing through all the knots and muscles of your stomach . . .

Feel your tension flowing . . .

All the way down your spine . . .

Down into the small of your back . . .

Down through your hips . . .

Buttocks . . .

Thighs . . .

Tension and anxiety just flowing

Down through your knees . . .

Legs . . .

Ankles and feet . . .

And then leaving your body through the tips of your toes . . .

Completely leaving your body through the tips of your toes.

Now go back through your body and breathe in relaxation to any part that still feels uptight . . .

Now bring *full* attention back to your breathing . . .

As you breathe in . . . and out through your nose . . .

Full attention to your breathing . . .

Noticing your breath . . .

Noticing whether it is warm or cool . . .

Whether you feel it more on one side of your nose than the other . . .

Don't try to change it.

Accept it just as it is. Is it deep? . . . or shallow? . . .

Rough or smooth?

Can you feel it on the skin outside your nose?

Just notice your breath . . .

Get to know all the characteristics of your breath for the next few minutes.

As thoughts come in . . . as they will . . . just notice them . . .

Without judging whether they are right or wrong . . .

Good or bad . . . just notice them

And V E R Y gently go back to your breathing.

It is very normal to have thoughts.

We all have them.

Thoughts . . . feelings . . . physical pain . . . itches . . . giggles . . .

All will come up.

Planning, past memories, emotions . . . all will come up as a natural process of this meditation . . .

Just accept what you see and feel and hear.

Notice it . . .

Bring *only* your awareness to it . . .

And then gently go back to your breathing.

Easily and effortlessly go back to your breathing . . .

See if you can feel your breath on the skin outside your nose.

Follow your breath as it begins to come in your nose, as it is going in, until it is completely in.

Then follow it as it begins to go out, as it is going out, until it is completely out.

Spend a few minutes now . . .

Quietly meditating . . .

Quietly bringing your full attention to your breathing.

Spend a few minutes knowing that every time you breathe in . . .

You are breathing in *powerful positive* energy . . .

And as you breathe out, you are letting go . . .

Letting go of all negativity . . . tension . . . anxiety . . .

Making space for more positive energy to come in.

Spend a few minutes bringing your full attention to your breathing.

Know that whatever comes up is perfect.

Just very gently, without judgment.

Continue to come back to your breath . . .

Always coming back to your breathing when anything takes you away from it.

Stay in this place for as long as you wish and when you are ready, count to five and open your eyes.

Special Symbols

When you take time to do your regular daily meditations, you can take time to relax your entire body and quiet your mind.

There will be other times when you will want to go into your special place or just relax so that you can do visualizations and affirmations without meditating first. It will be necessary to feel relaxed so that these exercises can be as effective as possible. Once you get used to the process of meditation, it will become easier and easier to relax at will.

For example, if you are standing in line in the bank, late for an appointment, and feel yourself getting irritated and uptight at the apparent powerlessness of the situation, you can bring your attention to your breathing and relax. As you bring your attention to your breath, as it goes in and goes out of your nose, you can feel peace and relaxation flow through your entire body. You get in a new habit of responding with relaxation when you bring your attention to your breath.

Another way of relaxing at will is to visualize a symbol that means relaxation to you. For example, a gently soaring seagull flying high in the sky, or a sailboat drifting on the distant horizon. One person I know uses a waterfall.

Find a symbol that makes you feel peaceful.

Close your eyes and let yourself picture that symbol.

Let peace and relaxation flow through your entire body. Feel the peace.

Keep this symbol for as long as you want it. Change it or vary it whenever you wish. The main point is that it will take you to a state of relaxation that works for you.

Inner Sanctuary Meditation

Now . . . I will guide you to your very special place . . . your inner sanctuary . . . *your safe place.*

Now I am going to guide you to a very special place inside . . .

A place where you are absolutely safe . . . a place where you have all your truth . . . all your answers.

You are going to find a place within that you knew from the past when you were happy

Or you can create a new place . . .

A place that has everything that you want and

Everything that you need.

This can be near the ocean or the forest,

Near a lake or the mountains . . .

Anywhere you would like to be where you are perfectly safe . . .

A place where no harm can come to you . . .

Where you can find your truth . . .

Your answers . . .

Your peace . . .

Now begin to bring your attention again to your breathing.

Bring your full attention to your breathing

As you breathe in and breathe out.

This time know that you are breathing in powerful golden energy. Every time you breathe in, you are breathing in powerful positive healing energy.

And every time that you breathe out, you are letting go . . .

Making more room for this positive golden energy to come in and circulate all around you . . .

Inside and out . . .

Healing . . .

Energizing . . .

Warming . . .

Find yourself on a spiral staircase inside that goes down to your special safe place. In your imagination, take your shoes off so that you can feel the steps beneath your feet. What are they made of? Are they carpeted? How do they feel?

Put out your hand on the railing and feel what it is made of.

What color?

Size?

Shape?

Feel yourself going deeper and deeper . . .

Going deeper and deeper to a very special place inside of you. As the steps get wider and wider . . .

As you go deeper and deeper . . .

You might find that you are getting a bit lighter . . .

Feeling just a bit lighter.

Your left hand . . .

Or maybe your right hand might be a little tingling . . .

Maybe your fingertips . . .

Or your toes . . .

Might feel a bit numb.

Maybe not.

That's okay . . . either way . . .

As you get to the bottom . . .

Make sure that your shoes are off so that you can feel the ground beneath your feet . . .

You are on a path to your special place

Notice what time of year it is . . .

Are there any special sounds? . . .

Smells? . . .

Feel the breeze as it blows along your skin and through your hair . . .

Find your special place and make sure that you have everything you want in it.

It can be indoors or outdoors . . .

Or maybe both . . .

Anything you want . . . any place you feel good in . . .

Know that this is your place.

No one else can ever come here unless you invite them.

Spend a few minutes getting comfortable in your special place.

Spend a few minutes letting yourself feel good about yourself in your special place.

Let yourself feel very good about yourself in your special place.

Know that you deserve to feel good about yourself.

Now . . .

Continue to meditate for a few moments in your special place.

Inner Guide Meditation

Deep within all of us lives our own truth . . . Now that you know that you have a special place within you where you can always go, feel safe and find peace, special answers will soon be yours.

Deep within you, in your special place, lies your inner knowledge . . . intuition . . . inner knowing. It is yours and you are the only one who can find it. Inside your special place lives an Inner Guide, who can be called your Inner God or Goddess, a Special Friend, a Sponsor, a Spirit Guide . . . or any other name that makes you feel comfortable. I will call her an Inner Goddess. You can just substitute your own name whenever you choose. Your Inner Goddess has always been there.

Bring yourself to your special place and notice that there is a hallway that you did not see before. It is enveloped in bright light!

Walk over to the threshold of the doorway . . .

Look out . . .

Be relaxed . . .

You are in your safe place . . .

Let the feelings of peace and trust pour all over you.

Quietly . . . slowly . . .

Bring in good feelings about yourself.

Your Inner Goddess is walking slowly toward you through the golden light. Her form is gradually appearing before you.

Can you see what she is wearing?
What she looks like?
Can you make out the features on her face?
Reach out your hand in welcome.
Walk slowly back with her to your special place.
Be welcoming and thank her for being there for you.
Ask her if she has a name. Tell her yours.
Is there anything you would like to tell her?
Ask her?
Does she have a gift for you?
Do you have one for her?
Stay as long as you like here and know that she is always with you.
You can come back and meet her anytime you wish.
You will always find special, healing energy and love with her.
Whenever you are ready, come back to your room, your awake state.
Just be sure you count to five before you open your eyes.

18

The Power Of Affirmations

Thoughts of your mind have made you what you are and thoughts of your mind will make you what you become from this day forward.

Catherine Ponder

The practice of meditation quiets our mind and develops our awareness of what is going on in the moment. It opens us to the reality of the moment. Our awareness grows and we are able to hear how we talk to ourselves. This is our self-talk. The concepts of self-talk and affirmations are explained more fully in my first book, *The Journey Within: A Spiritual Path To Recovery.*

As we quiet our minds and listen to our self-talk, we begin to see that the words we tell ourselves have the power to make us feel good or bad, confident or fearful, positive or negative, even healthy or sick. As we have learned, until we know better what we say to ourselves, we are conditioned by our perceptions of our past experiences.

Once we realize that how we feel is often a direct result of how we talk to ourselves, then we have a new and powerful tool to change how we feel. We then come to another crossroad . . . another moment of choice . . . another place of volition.

How do you choose to feel?

Remember that this self-talk can be broken down into four parts:

1. Consciousness
2. Perception
3. Sensation

— — — — — *volition* — — — — — —

4. Reaction

Volition lies between the third and fourth part. Here is our moment of choice.

Without this knowledge, without knowing how to stop the reaction or at least change the reaction to a pleasant one, we can get locked into negative behavior patterns.

For example, because of my positive experiences with meditation, affirmations and visualizations, I began some classes for people in recovery. They had wonderful results. One beautiful sunny day while driving with my convertible top down, I suddenly had a clear vision of a gold thread reaching from the center of my body far up into the blue sky. Suddenly I knew that I was to teach meditation to larger audiences around the country. There were no words. I suddenly just knew. My stomach immediately tightened with fear and I felt my breath become quick and shallow.

My reaction of fear came from my deeply embarrassing past experiences which resulted in my decision never to speak before a group of people.

Here I was, with what I thought to be a message from my Higher Power, my Higher Self, telling me that I was to go out into the world and speak. Other condemning self-talk followed.

"No one will want to hear you."

"You have nothing to say."

"*They* (meaning those out there already speaking) say it better than you anyway. *They* know how to do it. People want to hear *them*."

These messages came from my old tapes of never feeling good enough.

A few days after my first book, *Journey Within,* came out, my publisher called and asked:

"Do you speak?"

"No!" I answered quickly.

"Will you?"

"No."

"Why don't you think about it and call me back in two weeks?"

I didn't call him back.

Three weeks later he called me and said that I was on the program to speak at a conference in Albany in three months. The next months were agony for me. Every time I thought of the upcoming event, my stomach tightened and my palms became sweaty. My self-talk continued with the same negative messages.

Nineteen days before the conference, I realized that I had not done any affirmations. Affirmations are positive words that we say to ourselves, whether we believe them or not. I had been teaching the Power Of Affirmations to my classes and many people had achieved powerful changes in their lives because of them. Affirmations work when they are written 10 times a day for 21 days. With only 19 days left and hoping it would be enough, I wrote:

I am a dynamite, confident, motivating speaker.

Not believing a word of it and feeling like a phoney, I wrote it 10 times a day for 19 days. I remembered the phrase, "Fake it 'till you make it," and let myself feel the power of the words flow through my body. Each time fear came up, I would say this affirmation. I wrote it on a card and carried with me. I put it on the visor of my car.

While still nervous when it finally came time to speak, my nervousness was nothing like it was before doing the affirmations. Repeating these words again before speaking, I felt the power of the words flow through me.

I continued writing this message to myself before other speaking dates, feeling the powerful effect of the words. I still do get nervous, but for just a few minutes now. I am actually at the place where I enjoy speaking and look forward to it.

Before doing affirmations, my self-talk of "I am not good enough" came into my consciousness. I perceived this, I heard this in my mind. The sensation of fear arose. I judged this sensation as unpleasant. My reaction to this feeling was that I wanted to stop it and I wanted it to go away. I did not want to feel fear.

Later, when I became aware of the negative self-talk that led to the feeling of fear, I could just note the fear without judgment and replace the negative self-talk with a positive affirmation.

When we open our awareness to the present, we learn to be at choice. Affirmations are powerful tools that help us to break free from our past messages. Many people use affirmations today to change their lives. Many therapists who have experienced the positive value of affirmations in their own lives have recommended them to their clients.

Affirmations are so simple that many people think they are too simple to work! Try them for just 21 days and witness for yourself the miraculous changes that happen in your life.

The 4 Basic Ingredients Of Affirmations

Positive

Affirmations must be positive. If you want to feel confident, for example, say,

"I am a confident person today!"

Do not say: *"I am no longer negative."*

Powerful

When you say your affirmation, say it with feeling. Let yourself F E E E L the power of the words. For example,

"I am a confident person today!"

Use the power of all your senses.

Think it. Hear your thoughts.

Feel it. Write it so you can feel it with your hands. Feel the pen or pencil in your hand or the computer or typewriter keys with your fingertips.

Write it 10 times a day for 21 days.

Hear it. Say it aloud.

Smell it. Be aware of the smell of the paper, the ink or the computer or typewriter.

In The Present

Say: ***"I am a confident person today!"***

Not: *"I will be a confident person!"*

Possible

The affirmation must be possible. I could not affirm that I am a famous singer because I am too tone deaf to have that be a reality. It is possible that I can be a successful writer.

What We Think Is Best For Us Is Not Always Best For Us

Shakti Gawain, author of *Creative Visualizations,* wrote that when completing our affirmation, we should either write, know or say that this (our affirmation) or something better for all concerned is manifesting itself for me. It is not always true that we know what is best for ourselves and if we learn to wait and listen, the right answer will be there.

Affirmations Saved An Over-Spender!

I received a call recently from a young woman who had attended one of my workshops. She told the following story:

She had become out of control with her spending and had been too afraid to tell anyone. Packages were hidden under her bed, never looked at once they were home. Closets were full of new unworn clothes. She would go to the store for a pair of shoes, see three pairs she liked, want them all and easily rationalize that she needed them all. If she were depressed or upset or felt anything she didn't want to feel, shopping gave her the adrenaline rush she needed, or thought she needed, to get through the rough time, to change her mood. She was close to deep trouble financially and she was physically sick with worry and shame.

She had never shared this obsession with anyone for fear they would try to stop her. She thought she was not ready to give up the behavior. However, after my workshop, she quietly began to write 10 times a day:

"I have everything I need today."

After a few days, some friends called and asked her if she wanted to go shopping. They went to the mall and looked at the new fall clothes.

"Isn't that stunning!" one friend said to her.

"Yes," she responded quietly, "but I have everything I need today." She couldn't believe she had said this!

A few days later she went shopping for a new bedroom set. She saw beautiful furniture at bargain prices. Each time she looked at a new suite, the words would just come to her unsummoned and she would surprise herself by saying:

"I have everything I need today."

She continued to write her affirmation until she completed 21 days. In the end she was able to talk about her addiction to her husband and, in time, she put her finances back in order.

I hear stories like this all the time. Lives changed with the use of affirmations! They can be used for many purposes. For example, when I feel too busy and I find myself saying, "I'll never get everything done," I can affirm:

"God gives me all the time I need to do God's will today."

or

"All the energies of the universe are guiding me to my next step."

Some Examples Of Positive Affirmations

"I am terrific just the way I am!"
"I am attracting positive people to me today!"
"I eat healthy food to keep me at a healthy weight."
"I am lovable and loving!"

You can use your affirmations anytime and anywhere. They can be independent of meditation or combined with meditation. They are powerful either way.

It can be very helpful to make a tape of your affirmations. Meditate for as long as you wish, bring yourself to your special place inside and then play your affirmation tape. This helps to imprint your affirmations into your subconscious.

Now write your own affirmations
and become the author of your own life script!

19

THE HEALING POWER OF SPIRITUALITY

When a person has had a Spiritual Awakening, the most important meaning of it is that they have now become able to do, feel and believe that which they could not do before on their unaided strength and resources alone. They have been granted a gift which amounts to a new state of consciousness and being. They have been set on a path that tells them that they are really going somewhere, that life is not a dead end, not something to be endured or mastered.

Adapted from
The 12 Steps and
12 Traditions

One day, while driving back to work after completing an errand, I became aware of a knot of fear rushing through my stomach. I have no idea what thought precipitated that fear. It was four o'clock in the afternoon and I suddenly realized that this was the first time all day that I had felt that feeling. I felt a rush of joy pour over me and a wide grin spread over my face. For as long as I could remember, that feeling of fear had lived in my stomach. This was the first day that I knew that fear by its absence. On this day I was aware that I had been free of it until 4 o'clock. I had been in recovery around three years at that time and it was a loud affirmation that recovery was working in my life.

On another clear crisp day in October, many years later, I was driving to work down the same street when suddenly, from seemingly nowhere, the poem I had written when 17 years old when came to mind:

"There is something I have to do . . .
And urge eating deep inside me; . . . "

I had written this poem at the age of 17, as I struggled to find out who I was and what life was all about. I was still desperately searching 17 years later when I was 34 when I went to the psychiatrist, in the depths of my alcoholism, still struggling and pleading for help.

"Will I be the same at 51?" I had asked, begging the doctor to take away my pain.

Somewhere from deep inside me on this 17-year cycle, my poem resurfaced.

It was 17 years later.

I realized I was 51 on this beautiful, bright and clear October day! At last I had a purpose. I knew I was at peace. I knew I was free!

What Is Spirituality?

Spirituality is such a personal thing. Spirituality is so personal, I will not even attempt to define it for you. Each of us reaches inside for our own truth to find where we are in each moment. We form our own definitions.

Along my own path of recovery I had a spiritual awakening. I became willing to acknowledge a power greater than myself in my life. I learned from those who had been on this path before me.

Spirituality is not religious but religion can be spiritual.

You do not have to believe in the masculine traditional God we are taught about in temples and churches to be spiritual but you can believe in that God and be spiritual.

You can even be an agnostic and be spiritual.
It all depends on how you define spirituality.
To me spirituality is what we experience when . . .

- we are connected with God's will for us.
- when we know we are aligned with our Higher Power.
- when we reach our highest good.
- when we come from our heart.
- when we come from good and love.
- Spirituality is the way we feel when we are other-centered rather than self-centered.
- Spirituality is an energy that comes to us when we reach out to someone else . . . an aliveness, an awakening, an enlightment.
- We feel spiritual when we let go . . . when we make light of . . . when we forgive.
- It is that intangible feeling we have when we can see our character defects and still love ourselves . . .
- It's how we feel when we can see someone we love with all their character defects and look at them with a smile . . . And harder yet, when we look at the character defects in someone we do not respect or someone we do not like with the eyes of compassion and acceptance.
- When we act on spiritual principles, we feel bigger and fuller and better.
- It is what makes life worth living and is available to all of us, at all times. It is sometimes as hard to find as a needle in a haystack or as hard to practice as moving a mountain. Yet at other times it's right there at our fingertips, as easy as breathing, as easy as smiling at a new born baby, a rainbow or a sunset.
- It can be as big as a feeling of connectedness to all people, animals, the earth, the universe and God, or as right as a connectedness with one other person.
- It is that feeling we have when we know we have had a good day and we settle in under the blankets, feel the pillow soft under our head and say thank you to some unknown, mysterious, powerful and loving spirit other than ourselves.

Know that wherever you are in your recovery, you are at least one step ahead of the person behind you who is still suffering. Know that the power of your experience, compassion and love does make a difference. The power of the healing energy that begins within you is limitless. Reach out your hand to those behind you who want what you have. Reach your hand up to those in front of you to get what they have. Each and every one of us is an essential link in the healing of the universe.

20

METTALOVINGKINDNESS

Waking from sleep is awakening.
Waking up from ignorance is enlightenment.
Enlightened people are those who have awareness
in life, who are free from psychological sleep,
whatever they are doing.

Dhiravamsa
The Way of Non-Attachment

There is a wonderful Buddhist meditation called ***LOVING-KINDNESS.*** I have adapted it for people in recovery. It is really healing for all people because we are all recovering from whatever has blocked us in the past from being fully alive today. It is particularly healing for people in any kind of recovery.

It is a powerful way we can all contribute to peace in the universe. It had been said by many that if more and more people meditate for world peace, it will happen. It *is* happening. And we are all a part of it.

Gently close your eyes and bring your attention to your breathing as you breathe in and out from your nose.

Breathing in positive and loving energy . . .

Breathing out tension and resentments and negativity . . .

Breathing in peace

Breathing out resistance . . .

Feel your connectedness with your body touching the floor, rug, pillow or chair.

Feel your connectedness as you become aware of clothes touching your body, your hands at any point of contact.

Let your entire body relax as you feel all your stress and tension pour out from the tips of your fingers and the tips of your toes.

Now gently bring yourself to your special place.

Bring yourself to the safety of your special place.

After you have become quiet and peaceful, bring your attention to that special part of you, in your center, where you feel L O V E. Spend a few minutes gently breathing in and out, and bring your attention to that place of L O V E, usually found in the center of your chest or where you picture your heart lives. Bring in thoughts of L O V E and send them to your heart.

Let yourself F I L L with thoughts and feelings of L O V E. This can work easily if you let yourself think of someone you do love or picture love coming into you.

Now be with this feeling and say to yourself quietly:

May I be happy . . . May I be peaceful . . .
May I be free from suffering.
May I be whole and healed.
May I come from a place of love and peace.
May I continue to find my special gifts.
May I continue to follow my purpose.
May I be free.
May I be open to truth and love and pass it on.

Let yourself F E E L these words as you speak them quietly and lovingly to yourself. *Act as if* . . . even if you don't feel that this makes sense at first.

May I be happy . . . May I be peaceful . . .
May I be free from suffering.
Happy . . . peaceful . . . free from suffering . . .
Always living in a place of love and peace

Now bring someone into your heart who you care about and say,

May you be happy
May you be peaceful
May you be free from suffering.
May you find your special gifts and your purpose.

May you be whole and healed.
May you come from a place of love and peace.
May you be free.
May you be happy . . . peaceful . . . free from suffering
May you be open to truth and love
And pass it on.

Now, if you can and if you want to, bring someone in you would like to come to peace with, someone you would like to have a healing relationship with, someone you might need to forgive or someone you would like to receive forgiveness from and say,

May you be happy May you be peaceful
May you be free from suffering.
May you find your special gifts and your purpose.
May you be whole and healed.
May you come from a place of love and peace.
May you be free.
May you be happy . . . peaceful . . . free from suffering
Now let's extend this feeling to your family and friends,
May everyone in my life be happy May you be peaceful.
May you be free from suffering.
May everyone find their special gifts . . . their purpose.
May you be whole and healed.
May you come from a place of love and peace.
May you be free.
May you be happy . . . peaceful . . . free from suffering.

And now to all people who are still suffering from addictions, compulsions and dependencies, for ACoAs and for people who grew up in dysfunctional homes, for people with AIDS and other life-threatening diseases, to people who are in wars and for people who are hungry and homeless:

May everyone be happy May everyone be peaceful
May everyone be free from suffering.
May everyone find their special gifts . . . and their purpose.
May everyone be whole and healed.
May you come from a place of love and peace.
May you be free.
May you be happy . . . peaceful . . . free from suffering
May you be open to truth and love
And pass it on.

And finally spend a few minutes feeling this love expand from yourself to all beings, absolutely knowing that the P O W E R of these positive thoughts and feelings have powerful, positive qualities far exceeding our comprehension. Healing miracles are taking place at this very moment as a direct result of this meditation.

Our recovery is helping others recover.

We are transforming our pain into gifts, our past into presents!

Appendix I

Specific Meditations for Healing

The following guided meditations and visualizations are all for specific purposes, such as making changes in your life or easing anxiety. It is helpful to begin always with a few moments of meditation to get centered. You can do this by first going into your inner sanctuary, bringing in your inner guide and meditating. Or you can meditate first, then go into your inner sanctuary and bring in your inner guide. Find whichever way works best for you.

Releasing Your Endorphins For Healing Pain

Meditate for as long as you wish to get centered. Once you feel peaceful and quiet, go into your inner sanctuary and then bring in your inner guide.

Now sit for a few moments in your special place, letting yourself feel what's going on in your body.

Let yourself be aware of any pain that is there.

This can be either emotional or physical pain.

Now imagine what your endorphins might look like. I like to picture them as little red hearts with big smiles, eager to be used. You can use this or any other positive picture that makes you feel comfortable.

Once you have a picture of your endorphins, imagine that they have been stored in a place in your head for a long, long time, just waiting

APPENDIX I

SPECIFIC MEDITATIONS FOR HEALING

The following guided meditations and visualizations are all for specific purposes, such as making changes in your life or getting unstuck. It is helpful to begin always with a few moments of meditation to get centered. You can do this by first going into your inner sanctuary, bringing in your inner guide and meditating. Or you can meditate first, then go into your inner sanctuary and bring in your inner guide. Find whichever way works best for you.

Releasing Your Endorphins For Healing Pain

Meditate for as long as you wish to get centered. Once you feel peaceful and quiet, go into your inner sanctuary and then bring in your inner guide.

Now sit for a few moments in your special place, letting yourself feel what is going on in your body.

Let yourself be aware of any pain that is there.

This can be either emotional or physical pain.

Now imagine what your endorphins might look like. I like to picture them as little red hearts with big smiles, eager to help me. You can use this or any other positive picture that makes you feel comfortable.

Once you have a picture of your endorphins, imagine that they have been stored in a place in your head for a long, long time, just waiting to be released! Imagine that they have been locked inside a closet, just waiting to help you.

What does that closet door look like?

What color is it?

Imagine that the door has a lock on it.

Picture the lock . . . and size, shape, texture and color that you wish . . .

Now create in your mind a powerful key . . . any size, shape, texture and color that you wish . . .

Place the key in the lock

And open the door.

Let all the endorphins flow out!

Releasing New Energies For Change

The purpose of this guided meditation is for you to move further along on your self-discovery journey and to clear your path to find your special gifts and your highest purpose in this present time. As we move forward on our path and become closer to our Higher Power, we become more aware of the changes that need to be made in our lives. We're moving toward peace and serenity, and our highest purpose, and our highest good.

When we allow ourselves to feel what we really feel and then accept it, feelings lose their negative power to damage us. They are transformed into positive healing energy.

Change is often thought of as a fearful and difficult time. Because it has been that way in the past, we think it will continue to be that way. But with the tools of meditation, visualizations and affirmations, it can, instead, be a very exhilarating, energizing and satisfying time . . . a deep and spiritual time.

So many of the tools that we used to survive in early childhood are no longer appropriate in our lives today. We need to look at what we have been carrying with us for so long and make decisions about what is no longer useful. This will be a time for self-exploring and, with the help of your inner guide, you can then find your path to change. This is good for anyone who wishes to grow and change, to become more spiritual, to become closer to a Higher Power.

Those of us who have come from our own alcoholism, drug or any other addictions, or from families of addiction or dysfunction, have had our own pain and suffering. As we reach our bottom and surrender, knowing we are powerless, we're on the path of recovery. We're coming home.

On this special trip we carry with us the memories of our past. It is as if our minds are like a vast library, storing all the volumes and volumes of books, journals, notebooks and slips of paper of all our past experiences. But what is important to note is that we are actually carrying with us at all times our own perceptions and our own interpretations of these perceptions, feelings and emotions in our memories.

Each and every one of us has a higher purpose in this universe. But how do we find it? How do we know it?

First, we have to be quiet so we can see where we are in this moment.

We have to quiet our thoughts, quiet our minds so that we can see where we are right now. Meditation allows us to quiet our chattering minds.

Meditation brings us to that place of quiet. We can examine where we are on our path, put a light on the places that have kept us stuck and see what needs to be changed. We cannot change until we know where we are now. We cannot change until we see what there is to change.

Blocked emotions block energy. When we still have feelings stuck in our storehouse of memories, we are not able to be fully alive and experience the now.

Begin by meditating for as long as you wish . . . until you feel centered.

Whenever you are ready, go into your inner sanctuary . . .

You are on a path to your special place

Notice what time of year it is . . . Are there any special sounds? . . . Smells? . . . Feel the breeze as it blows along your skin and through your hair . . . Find your special place and make sure that you have everything you want in it. It can be indoors or outdoors . . . Or maybe both . . . Anything you want . . . any place you feel good in . . . know that this is your place. No one else can ever come here unless you invite them. Spend a few minutes getting comfortable in your special place. Spend a few minutes letting yourself feel good about yourself in your special place.

Let yourself feel v e r y good about yourself in your special place.

Know that you deserve to feel good about yourself.

Now . . . continue to meditate for a few moments in your special place.

Know how safe you are! Feel the safety . . . the security . . . the peace . . .

Deep within you . . . in your very special place lies your inner knowledge . . . intuition . . . inner knowing . . .

It is yours and you are the only one who can find it.

Welcome your Inner Goddess.

Look directly into the eyes of your inner guide. Ask her if she will help you, because we are going to take some time to look at different areas of your life where a change is needed for you to grow. You don't have to make many changes at all. In fact, just one is perfect for now . . . to help you get unblocked and energized. Take your Inner Goddess' hand and slowly walk to the doorway where she entered your special place. It is bathed in beautiful light. Walk through this doorway and feel the energy of the light throughout your entire body. Feel this light caress and love you as it circulates all around you, inside and out.

In front of you is your spiritual path.
Six smaller paths lead off to the left of the main path.
Each path is a part of your life.
There is a path for Spirituality.
One for family.
One for leisure and entertainment.
One for work.
One for health and exercise.
And one for relationships and social life.
On the right is a path for your life purpose.
Slowly walk down your Spiritual Path . . .

Stopping very quietly to look down each path on your left. Stop as long as you wish. Explore how you feel. Just let whatever comes up for you be there. Don't try to force anything or make it what you think it should be. Just be relaxed and free and be with your breathing.

If the path feels comfortable, move on to the next one.
If there is discomfort, look for the message.
Do the same with family, leisure, work, health, relationships.
One path will have a strong message for you.
Enter the path that feels the most uncomfortable . . .
Or . . .

Enter the path that has the change you need to handle right now in your life.

Remember, choose just one area . . . it could be a new job or more time with the kids, it could be going to school or writing a book . . .

One area . . .
One path is calling you.
Is it spiritual, family, leisure, work, health or relationships?

Stand before each path and wait quietly, with your Inner Goddess at your side.

If you don't hear any answers, don't be concerned. They will come in time. Know that you can come back to this part any time.

As you continue to practice meditating, you will become closer and closer to your Higher Power and your Inner Goddess . . . your intuition.

If you feel stuck in any way, ask your Inner Goddess to guide you. Ask your Higher Power to release any fear or resistance.

In making changes it is necessary to first explore, then discover, make a decision and then take an action step.

Make a decision now to make the changes that are needed in your life.

Make a decision now and walk down the path that needs to be changed.

Feel protected and safe, knowing that you are in your special place. Feel the energy of light protecting you. Feel the power of your breath as you breathe in and out of your nose.

Ask your Inner Gooddess for a symbol for this change.

Reach out as she places it into your hand.

What is the symbol?

What does it look like?

What size?

Shape?

Texture?

Color?

Make an affirmation now about your change.

Affirm that your change is happening easily and effortlessly.

Affirm that all the positive energy of the universe is guiding you with your change.

Imagine the change has already taken place.

Let good feelings of accomplishment pour over your entire body . . . recording in all your cells . . . in your DNA . . . positive powerful, healthy feelings are now being recorded.

Spend some time quietly meditating, quietly being where you are and accepting this new growth in your life.

Stay as long as you wish . . .

And whenever you are ready, come back to your awake state.

Just be sure to count to five before you open your eyes.

Jot down whatever is appropriate in your notebook.

Releasing Your Endorphins For Healing Disease

You can use your own imagination and play with this exercise for all physical and mental diseases. Many doctors are incorporating meditation and guided imageries in their treatment programs for cancer, AIDS and other diseases.

If you are experiencing serious illness, I strongly suggest that you find such a medical doctor and work closely with him or her. There have been numerous scientific documentations of people who have gone into spontaneous remissions or had years added to their lives. While not all people can recover physically, they can come to an inner peace in a spiritual recovery.

Getting Unstuck

This is a short meditation to help you get *unstuck*. There are times when we can't seem to move forward, when every day seems the same as the one before. There are times when we keep making the same mistakes and do not seem to learn from them. There are times when everyone around us seems to be moving forward but we are making no progress at all.

If this is where you are now right now, don't be hard on yourself! Remember that you are reaching new levels of consciousness. You are learning new tools to energize yourself and move forward. This is a process and it takes time. In fact, it takes a lifetime . . . which is why it is so exciting. We are always moving forward. There is always something new in front of us.

But when we are stuck, there is something hidden that we cannot see. There is something blocking our path. There is something blocking our positive energy. Know that your subconscious has the answers. You just have to reach out.

With faith and trust that this block will be revealed, get yourself comfortable and take your journey to your special place.

. . . Imagine yourself right now on a path . . . your life path . . .

If you turn around, you can look behind you at all you have done . . . you can see your entire life . . . from birth until this present moment . . .

Now look in front of you. Before you lie all the unknown moments of your future . . . adventures . . . relationships . . . everything that is going to take place. This is a path that you can't see until you get to each step.

Now imagine where you are right now, in this present moment . . .

Around you are enormous sacks of tools that you have been carrying . . . all your collections of everything that you have dragged, pulled, pushed and carried . . . surrounding you . . . engulfing you. You needed these tools at one time . . . to get you through rough and trying times. They no longer serve any purpose. They hold you back.

Push them aside as best you can . . . or climb over them . . . or around them. Do whatever you have to do to set yourself free . . . and step back and view them. The baggage is so high you cannot see your past over the pile . . . you can't see it clearly . . . you can't see it honestly.

Now look ahead . . . still attached to this mound of memories is a neon light flashing the word *fear.*

This is the place where we will work. This is the place we will examine . . . to find what you are still attached to that is holding you back.

Take all the time that you need.

Your inner guide is there for love and support and insight . . . so that you can look . . . examine . . . reevaluate and move forward! You are safe and can handle all that comes up for you at this present time.

Ask your inner guide to shine the light on your answers.

Ask for willingness . . .

To be willing to give up . . .

To let go of what no longer works for you.

Let go of what is no longer valuable or positive in your life today.

Spend a few moments in gratitude. Thank your Inner Guide for being there and know that she is always there for you.

Feel new energy surge through your body.

Feel the stuck places break up into small pieces . . . flowing through your body. Feel them begin to dissolve into smaller and smaller pieces, then melt into nothingness.

Whenever you are ready, come back to your room. Be sure to count to five before you open your eyes.

It would be helpful to write down what you found on your path at this time.

Taking Back Your Personal Power

As we have learned, words and images are very powerful. When we tell ourselves that we can't, then we probably can't. It's that simple. That feeling of powerlessness comes from our past experiences and we are bringing our past into our present to keep us stuck.

When we were not listened to in our childhood or when our thoughts and wishes were not validated, we felt powerless. When we are punished or ignored (which is certainly a form of punishment) or when we have done what we thought right even though it differs from someone who has authority over us, our personal feeling of power diminishes. These feelings are then stored within us and we take them with us in all the situations that we are in. When we feel threatened by an upcoming confrontation, our feelings of fear are triggered, our fight-or-flight instincts are aroused. Because of earlier bad experiences, our feelings of powerlessness come up and all we want to do is run away.

Giving in is a form of running away. Giving up is a form of running away. When we do not fight for ourselves, we are running away. We are shutting down. We are closing up. We are not letting our healthy energies flow freely and naturally.

After years of dealing in this way, we come to the point where we feel more and more powerless in most situations. We no longer argue. We no longer speak our own truth. We become people-pleasers and wimps. And we certainly don't feel very good about ourselves.

Many years ago, when my children were two, four and six, I experienced this feeling of powerlessness to such a deep extent that it stayed with me for many years.

One Sunday a relative came to the house bearing gifts. He insisted on a hug and kiss from each of the children. Judy said, as all normal two year olds would, "No!" This relative refused to give Judy her gift until she honored his request. She cried. He remained firm. No hug and kiss: no gift.

Judy ended up under the kitchen table sobbing her heart out. I remember the terrible struggle I went through in my mind. I wanted to yell at this relative and tell him to just give Judy the crayons. I wanted to scream at him and tell him to stop being so stubborn. But instead I held in all my feeling. I felt impotent. I didn't know why I couldn't speak up. I felt ashamed. I felt disloyal to my own daughter because I didn't want to cause a scene. I didn't want the confrontation. I was embarrassed that I had such feelings. I didn't know why I had them. I didn't know what was wrong with me.

Today I know that this was the result of years and years of feeling powerless. I feared arguments. I feared confrontations. I had lost all confidence and didn't feel I had the right to speak up.

The following is a powerful exercise to enable you to *take back your personal power!*

It will help you feel strong and energized. You will experience a complete change in how you handle disagreements and confrontations by just using it a few times.

Have a piece of paper and crayons or colored pencils nearby for this guided imagery.

Spend as much time as you want in meditation.

Then go into your special place and ask your inner guide to be there with you for love and support.

After you feel safe and centered, remember a time when you gave your power away. Remember a time when you gave up your power to someone else.

Sit quietly and think about that time.

Think about that person.

Know that you are absolutely safe and that no harm can come to you.

Know that with all the in breaths, you are breathing in all the healing and positive powers of the universe.

Know that with all the out breaths, you are releasing all anxiety, all tension, all fears.

If any fear does come up for you, let it be there.

What does it look like?

Where do you feel it in your body?

In your throat?

Stomach?

Gut?

Are your fists clenched?

Is your jaw clenched?

What color is your fear?

What size?

Shape?

Texture?

Put it in your hand and throw it away!

Sit for a few moments feeling the freedom, knowing that you can feel your fear and let it go. You can throw it away. You can drop it. You can let it go.

Now, when you are ready, invite the person in to whom you gave your power. If you would rather not bring that person into your safe, special place, create a new room outside that is surrounded by yellow protective light. No harm, no negative energy can come into this new room.

Welcome this person and thank her or him for coming to you.

Explain the nature of this visit.

Ask this person for your power back.

Make this request in a very firm, self-assured and confident voice.

Put your hand out with the clear knowledge that you will get your power back.

If need be, repeat your request and insist that it happens right now.

It is absolutely time to take back your personal power.

Ask for it back.

Firmly.

Strongly.

It is yours!

Hold on to it!

What does your personal power look like?

What size . . . ?

Color . . . ?

Shape . . . ?

Does it have an aroma?

A sound?

A texture?

Be with your power.

Feel your power!

Thank the other person and ask them to leave.

They have no power over you.

Go back to your special, safe place and let all the energy of your power flow through your entire body, circulating in every cell, in every DNA. It is yours forever!

Spend as long as you like and whenever you are ready, come back to the present.

Just be sure to count to five before you open your eyes.

When you have had a chance to adjust yourself to being back in your room, take your crayons and paper and draw a picture of your power.

Now . . .

Write the word *power* on a piece of paper and put it in your pocket.

Know that you always have your power with you.

This is very powerful. Whenever you are uncomfortable or wish to avoid a scene or confrontation, take your power with you in your pocket. You might want to use a crystal, stone or gem to symbolize your power. Do whichever makes you feel the strongest. Just know that it is there! Feel that it is there.

F E E E L that power.

It's yours!

Finding Your Special Gifts And Special Purpose

We will continue this personal journey to find your special gifts.

We will then continue your path to find your highest purpose for this time in your life.

To come to peace, we must look at all the patterns that we are carrying with us and discard the ones that bring us negativity, confusion and doubt. We must let go of the ones that block us from being one with our Higher Power.

We want to let go of the patterns that are no longer of any value, that are not appropriate today. We want to reinforce those which manifest harmonious relations and fulfill our highest creative potential, our highest good, our highest purpose . . .

Living in the past continues to bring us great pain.

Holding on to anger and resentments keeps us in an unhappy, unloving place in our present. When we hold on to the negative tapes that have kept us stuck, we cannot move forward. We cannot fulfill our highest good.

Our pain can serve a useful purpose if we are willing to let it go. The negative energy of pain can be transformed to powerful healing energy.

If we can see our pain and accept it, knowing that we cannot do anything about the past, but are willing to let it go today, we can bring compassion and love to ourselves. We can accept ourselves just as we are. As we are able to do this more and more, we will be able to accept others as they are and bring love and compassion to them.

Know that you are in your very special place inside your inner sanctuary. Imagine yourself surrounded by a powerful, healing yellow light. Take a moment to pray that any obstacles that block you from peace, good relations and freedom may become clear to you, and that we may transform them for the benefit of all.

Take
Time
To
Pray.

Feel your whole body radiate with this golden light. Feel yourself becoming lighter and lighter until you feel like a feather soaring in the wind. Let yourself land on your special path, becoming aware that there is a divine pattern in the universe underlying all existence. See before you another doorway radiating in golden light. Your spiritual guide, your Inner Goddess, is waiting for you to join her. Tell her that you have come in order to understand the nature of your mind, so that you may be healed and grow spiritually.

She now leads you into a new room. In this room is a single shelf with books that you have never seen. Reach up and take the book with your name on it. It is your book of life. Take this book with your name on it and find a place to sit where you are comfortable.

Now you can look at your life purpose, your skills and your gifts, and the means of actualizing your goals. Now you can see all the stages of your life that you want to look at . . . safely . . . protected . . . secure. If you find great suffering, you can take back your personal power, reclaim your life so that you may actualize your gifts. Notice times that you gave in to the will and expectations of others. Affirm that you never need to do that again. It is yours.

Now . . . light a candle so that you may see your gifts. First, find those patterns that you have outgrown . . . all thought forms . . . dependencies . . . character defects . . . all actions that are no longer appropriate in your life today . . . those that hinder your realization of your life's full potential.

Inside your book of life you will find a very, very thick page. This page is so thick that you cannot see through it. On it is recorded a time in your life which still causes you great shame.

It still causes you great pain.

It is a time that you have hidden from yourself and others.

It is a time that you do not want to look at.

But know that by acknowledging this time, you will find great freedom.

Know that there is nothing to fear on this page.

This page holds memories of things that happened in the past . . . things that, when looked at, will no longer be alive in the present.

The feelings are still alive because of your fear of seeing them.

As you allow yourself to look at this page,

Notice how it is getting lighter and lighter . . .

It is getting clearer and clearer.

See how it has no power over you.

As you allow yourself to see it, it becomes transparent and you can see the next page through it!

Finally!

You can see the page right under it that has been hidden for so long!

At last . . .

You can see your gifts!

The gifts that have been hidden to you because of your shame and guilt, your character defects.

What are your special gifts?

What is the special gift you have to pass down to others?

You have waited a *long* time to know what your gifts are!

Let yourself F E E E L the fullness and goodness of your gifts . . . of yourself!

F E E E L the joy of them!

Know that they are yours to pass on to others . . .

To share . . .

To feel the love of them . . .

To give them away . . .

To get them back!

Stay with these wonderful feelings for as long as you like and then . . . whenever you are ready, know that when this tape is finished, you will be taking them back with you to your special room. Know that these gifts are yours now . . .

Clear and bright . . .

Never to be buried and hidden again.

You have transformed your pain into presents . . . into gifts for yourself and others.

All these assets, strengths, all the gifts will be fully developed and are replacing your old patterns.

Now let the feelings of peace and freedom pour all over you. Give thanks to your Higher Power and your Inner Goddess for being with you and bringing you here.

Your Inner Goddess is now coming to take your hand.

She leads you to another doorway that is bathed in light.

Look out . . .

Your spiritual path is now wider . . .

You have come so far!

There is a fork a few hundred yards further on . . .

Notice how one of the roads curves down and is narrow while the other one is wide, curving upward . . .

A bright light is beckoning you . . .

Your spiritual guide, your Inner Goddess leads you on . . .

Safely . . .

Lovingly.

You reach the fork and are drawn magnetically to the light,

To the higher path . . .

To your purpose.

You look back and see how far you have come . . .

And of how much you have let go.

Stop for a moment

And be still.

Feel peace and gratitude . . .

Knowing your purpose for now is being made clear.
Your purpose is shining before you.
Quietly give thanks
And whenever you are ready
Come back to this room.
Just be sure you count to five before you open your eyes . . . the meditation is not over.
Very slowly get ready to open your eyes. Count slowly to five.
Open your eyes very, very slowly.
Take your notebook and think back and remember what path you took to make a change in your life. Was it spiritual?
Family? Leisure? Was it Work? Health? Relationships?
Give yourself some time to remember what it is you are going to change.
What is the decision you made?
What is one action step you can take to make that change a reality?
Now remember the purpose that was revealed to you and write it down.
Then write down the gifts that you found.
If there are some parts of this that you do not remember . . . just close your eyes and ask your Higher Power or your Inner Goddess for help. You can always rewind the tape to that place to refresh your memory. Take all the time you want right now to write down your thoughts and feelings. Turn the tape off until you are finished and then you can return to this tape for a short meditation to end this session.

Deepening Your Meditation

After you have been meditating a while and become comfortable with the basic meditation, there are more steps that you can take.

Increasing Your Time

By meditating for a longer period of time, you can deepen your meditation experience to become more centered. You will know when that time comes for you. You will have an inner urge to meditate longer. Follow it when that happens for you.

When I wanted to increase my meditation from 20 minutes to 30 minutes, I felt as if it would never happen. I would look at the clock every two or three minutes after 20 minutes and then every minute after 25 minutes. But I knew it was right and I stayed with it. I now meditate somewhere between 35 to 40 minutes in the morning and feel very comfortable with that at the moment.

There is a saying that goes, "We teach what we need to learn." While I was taking lessons in meditation, my meditation went well. Similarly when I teach meditation, I experience a great deal of satisfaction from meditating.

While I say that you cannot meditate wrong and while we are taught that wherever we are is perfect, there came a period for me when my mind would be off and running for an entire sitting period. I would be off in thinking or fantasy, not even knowing how long I had been away. I would suddenly realize this and bring myself back to my breathing, being as gentle and nonjudgmental of myself as possible.

People would tell me that they experienced this, too, and I would tell them that was fine. Just notice it and bring your attention back to your breathing. Some would say that it wasn't peaceful and that they weren't getting it. I would respond with the pat answers that they were getting it. Just notice it, I said, and go back to your breathing. You are training your mind. You are practicing. It is in the sitting, in the discipline, that the learning occurs. And this is all very true.

I have also been taught that when we want something we don't have, such as peaceful meditation or serenity, then we are suffering in our now. If we do not accept the now as it is, we suffer. When we accept what is going on in the moment, peace comes. It is the resistance to the now that creates our suffering.

Let go of resistance . . .

Enter peace!

But deep within me, where my truth lives, I had this nagging feeling that maybe there were other ways to experience the deeper meditation, finding that place of peace with more regularity. I wanted to find that as much as anyone else.

Going back to more sessions with my teacher, Larry Rosenberg, and reading more books such as *Seeking The Heart Of Wisdom* by Joseph Goldstein and Jack Kornfield, *Vispassana Meditation As Taught By Goenka* by William Hart and a number of wonderful books by Thich Nhat Hahn, I experimented with other ways to feel peace, additional ways to train my roaming mind to come back to my breathing. I also attended other retreats with other teachers, such as Joseph Goldstein and Sharon Saltzberg.

Some methods have worked more for me than others. Some work at some times more than at other times. I share them with you so that you may experience them for yourself and if you find them helpful, incorporate them into your own meditation.

It is important to keep in mind that meditation is to bring us closer to our truth, to peace, to our Higher Power. As we learn to quiet our minds, we are able to bring our attention to ourselves, accept ourselves just as we are and bring love and compassion to our self.

We can learn to accept ourselves just as we are with all our pluses and minuses! Once we accept ourselves, we can love ourselves with all of the wonderful gifts that we have along with our imperfections and our hangups.

Once we can love ourselves, once we can really F E E L love in our hearts, then we can bring the same love and compassion to others and make a difference in this world. We must know ourselves first. We must discover what it is in our lives that causes our suffering. By the practice of meditation, which is sitting regularly, sitting daily, we are able to bring this attention to the rest of our awakening hours. We are able to observe ourselves and learn from this observation.

Once we are able to observe our self-talk, those old tapes from the past that continue to run us, we are able to turn them around to new, positive and loving messages. We are able to learn to be in charge of our lives. We are able to learn to be actors instead of reactors . . . to discover the sources of our conditioning and become free from them.

Another very important lesson from meditation that you will begin to get more in touch with is impermanence. As you continue to watch the process of your breathing, you will see how nothing stays the same. While the breath might feel warm one time, that will change to cool, hot or cold at another time. While your breath might be smooth one time, it can change to rough, short or fast. Nothing remains the same.

This is also true of all of our moods, feelings and emotions. Once we know this, a new freedom comes to us. A new excitement! For once we know this, we will begin to lose the fear of our negative, unpleasant emotions.

For example, anger might scare you. But once you know that you can experience your anger, have your anger and watch your anger, it will pass away, then you no longer have to be afraid of your anger.

Or another time you might be bored. You don't have to fix it or fill the mood with something to take away the feeling of boredom. Once you know that everything is impermanent, then you can make your boredom an object of your meditation and watch it, examine it, be with it and watch it go away. Of course, the same is true with joy and happiness. They, too, pass on to something else . . . whatever the moment brings. So notice the impermanence. Notice the changes. You are learning to be fully alive in the moment.

Our minds are used to being busy and going off doing whatever they want to do. The process has been compared to a monkey, swinging from one tree to another . . . swinging here and there at every whim. Once we know this, how can we stop that monkey? How can we keep that monkey in one place? How can we keep that mind on one thing? How can we learn to concentrate?

Try A New Place Of Concentration

Follow your breath as it comes in and goes out of your nose or . . . focus on your chest as it rises and falls. Or if you have practiced yoga or another discipline, you might want to follow your breath through the entire process: entering your nose, . . . filling your chest . . . going down through your abdomen and then follow this process in reverse as the breath leaves your body.

Use whatever feels stronger to you, experimenting with them all and then making your decision. Stay with whatever process draws you to it.

But once the decision is made, please don't go back and forth. It becomes too much like the grass is always greener on the other side of the street. Or too much like the classic, "If I had that, I would feel better, or if I were over there, I would feel better. Or if she would just do this or if he would just do that, I would feel better."

Experiment with each way and then stay with the one you choose. Watching the process of your mind as it teases you, as it wants to go back to the way you didn't choose, or this way or that way. "Just one more time! Just one more and I'll feel better! If I do it that way, it will be better!"

There is so much to learn here and we can learn just by watching our own minds go back and forth. We can watch our bodies and our feelings react and respond to the mind going back and forth.

Another important lesson here is that as you get to know yourself better, as you are more in tune with your mind/breath/body process, you will begin to be able to identify changes in your body and breath as they begin to happen.

It is very exciting when you can connect the thought that preceded the feeling. In other words, if you notice your breathing change and become faster or slower, or if you are holding your breath, not breathing at all, identify the thought that preceded this reaction.

What a wonderful lesson in self-awareness when we learn for ourselves, not just read in a book, that our thoughts are responsible for how we feel. At this point of realization, just notice the thought *without judgment*. Just notice the thought and make a mental note of it.

Here are a series of exercises to keep your mind busy so that it won't run off like that monkey. Our minds are used to being free and undisciplined, jumping anywhere they want. By giving your mind a little something to do, you can still detach from yourself as if you were a gentle witness watching yourself. Your mind will have something to keep it busy until you are centered.

These exercises are not a substitute for quiet meditation. They are exercises to help you focus, help you to concentrate on the process of your breath.

Noting

Spend a few moments being with your breath, whether you are with the breathing in and out from your nose, the rising and falling of your chest or the filling and emptying of the full breath.

Follow your breath. If you are paying attention to your breathing at your nose, make a mental note of *in* as it goes in, and *out* as it goes out.

Every time you breathe in and out, make a mental note of *in* and *out.* Feel it where you are most drawn . . .

To the skin outside your nose or to the breath as it is coming in and going out or both. Where do you feel it? And notice how it changes. You might first feel it on the skin outside your nose and then not feel it there at all.

Notice the impermanence. Notice the changes.

Where do you feel it?

In and . . .

Out.

In . . .

Out.

If you are keeping your awareness with your chest . . . do the same thing . . .

Make a mental note of your chest rising and falling.

Notice all the sensations of your breath as it expands and contracts your chest.

Notice the impermanence.

Notice all the changes.

Simply make a mental note of rising as your chest expands and

Falling as it empties . . .

Rising and falling.

Rising.

Falling.

Or

If you bring your attention to your entire breath as it enters and leaves your body . . . just make a mental note of entering and leaving as it comes in and goes out.

Follow all the parts of your body as you feel your breath entering and leaving.

Bring your awareness to all the sensations and changes that you feel as you make a mental note. Notice the impermanence. Notice the changes.

Entering and

Leaving.

Entering.

Leaving.

Stay here with your breath as long as you wish.

Anchoring

Begin by being with your breath.

Be with your breath.

Bring your full attention to the places where your hands connect with your body . . .

Feel the skin of your right hand and where it is connecting.

Now feel the skin of your left hand and where it is connecting.
Are your fingers touching each other?
Are your hands warm . . .
Or cool?
Do you feel a fabric? A texture?
Is it hard or soft? Rough? Smooth? Or what?

You can stay in this place for as long as you wish or you can bring your awareness to any place of your body where it connects with the floor, the cushion or the furniture.

Feel that connection.

Feel at one with what you are connected to.

You might come to the place where you are no longer able to differentiate between the space you are connected to and your body.

Now bring your awareness to your clothes touching your body . . .
To any area that calls you first . . .
How does the piece of clothing feel on your body?
What temperature is it?

You can always come back here at any point of your meditation when you feel you need centering . . . when your mind is wandering and playing a game of its own.

Be here as long as you wish.

Counting

Counting can be practiced in a few ways. First, every time you breath in or out, think:

In, one . . . out, one

In, two . . . out, two . . . etc., until you get to five and then come back and begin again at one. Be with each breath and count each breath. If your attention is with your chest as it rises and falls, say to yourself:

Rise, one . . . fall, one

Rise, two . . . fall, two . . . etc., until you get to five and then begin again at one.

If your attention is with your full breath, just do the same with entering and leaving.

Entering . . . one
Leaving . . . one
Entering . . . two
Leaving . . . two . . . and so on.

Every time your mind takes you away from your counting, begin again until you feel centered and quiet and then be quietly with your breathing.

Mantra

Next try using a mantra and see how that works for you. Choose a word such as God, Moses, Buddha, Jesus, Allah, Higher Power, or any other words you want. You can choose a phrase such as "let go" or "letting go." Repeat the words or phrase over and over with each in and out breath. Do this until you are centered and quiet.

OM

Over the centuries, ***OM*** has been known as the universal sound that resonates in the deepest parts of ourselves. The vibrations from humming or sounding ***OM*** is said to clear our energy centers of all impurities and pressures.

Positive Words

Positive words and phrases help you to become centered. You can imagine breathing in peace and letting out tension, breathing in love and letting out resentment. Breathe in positive energy, letting out all negativity. Or use other phrases that would appeal to you.

Spend enough time to be comfortable with the idea of sitting and getting centered. This could take a week or a couple of weeks or even months. Continue to practice with the exercises that we just used. You might want to try others that you create for yourself. Once you feel comfortable with this, you can move on to another phase of your meditation.

Deepening Your Personal Insight

This next exercise is about spending time being with whatever comes up that takes you away from your breath so that you can learn from it. It becomes your focus of meditation.

For example, if you have been sitting and find that you have a feeling of concern come up over a future meeting with your boss, be with that feeling of concern.

Examine it.

Don't try to change it.

Just be with it.

What does it feel like?

Where do you feel it in your body?

What does it do to your breathing?

To your peace of mind?

What was the thought that preceded the feeling? When all this passes, come back to your breath.

When something else comes up . . . maybe a memory of something pleasant that happened yesterday . . . be with that feeling. What does *pleasant* feel like? Where do you feel it in your body? Does it have a size . . . shape . . . color? Again . . . don't get caught up with the feelings. Watch them, as from a distance and as they fade away, come back to your breath as it comes in and out of your nose, or as your chest rises and falls, or as your breath enters and leaves your body.

After a period of weeks or months, when you feel comfortable with this process, there is another step you may wish to take.

Uncovering

There may be times when you wish to directly examine a feeling and get to the root of a particular feeling. Again, for example, you may have a fear of a meeting with your boss. Meditate, get yourself centered and peaceful, bring yourself to your special place and imagine this conversation taking place.

Feel the feelings that you are having.
Examine the feelings as you have been doing.
Let these feelings flow all over you.
Know that you can handle these feelings.
That they do not need to have power over you.
Stay with your feelings and watch them disappear.
Know that they will disappear when the conversation actually happens.
Know that they are impermanent and that they have no power over you.
Experience the feelings until they go away and then gently go back to your breathing.

These exercises will bring you new insights. They will help you move into deeper meditations. Remember . . . you cannot meditate wrong. Meditate regularly, at least once each day. Develop a regular time and place. Eventually expand the time of your meditation to a longer period. You will know when it is time to do this. Trust yourself. Do this for yourself! Take the time that you need to meditate and watch your life change for the better, your world get bigger, your life become filled with love and peace.

You will grow more and more into the person you always wanted to be and become the very best that you are.

Know that you deserve nothing less than that.

Watch your energy expand as you feel love and compassion more and more of the time.

Watch as your path becomes clearer and new directions open up in your life. Your purpose will continue to unfold for you as you struggle less and less to know what is good and right for you!

Remember: Not one person that I know of who meditates regularly has picked up a drink or a drug again!

Appendix II

Resources

Addicts And Family Of Addicted

Al-Anon, Al-Anon Adult
Children of Alcoholics and
Alateen Family Groups
P.O. Box 862 Midtown Station
New York, NY 10018-086

Alcoholics Anonymous
Box 459
Grand Central Station
New York, NY 10163

Adult Children of Alcoholics
6381 Hollywood Blvd.,
Suite 685
Hollywood, CA 90028

Cocaine Anonymous
P.O. Box 1367
Culver City, CA 90232

Cult Awareness Network
2421 W. Pratt Blvd., Suite 1173
Chicago, IL 60645

Drugs Anonymous
P.O. Box 473, Ansonia Station
New York, NY 10023

Nar-Anon
P.O. Box 2562
Palo Verdes, CA 90274

Nar-Anon Family Groups
350 5th Street, Suite 207
San Pedro, CA 90731

Pill-Anon Family Programs
P.O. Box 120 Gracie Station
New York, NY 10028

Pills Anonymous
P.O. Box 473, Ansonia Station
New York, NY 10023

Co-dependents Anonymous —
Central Office
P.O. Box 5508
Glendale, AZ 85312

National Association for Adult
Children of Alcoholics
31582 Coast Highway, Suite B
Laguna Beach, CA 92677

Families

Caregivers Support Groups
Community Care Resources
(612) 642-4046
Wilder Foundation

Divorce Anonymous
P.O. Box 5313
Chicago, IL 60680

Families Anonymous
P.O. Box 344
Torrance, CA 90501
(P.O. Box 528
Van Nuys, CA 91409)

Parental Stress Service, Inc.
154 Santa Clara Ave.
Oakland, CA 95610

Parents Anonymous
22330 Hawthorne Blvd.
Torrance, CA 90503

Parents Without Partners
7910 Woodmont Ave.
Washington, DC 20014

Family Violence

Batterers Anonymous
P.O. Box 29
Redlands, CA 92373

Survivors Network
18653 Ventura Blvd., #143
Tarzana, CA 91356

Eating Disorders

Overeaters Anonymous
4025 Spenser Street,
Suite 203
Torrance, CA 90503

Food Addicts Anonymous
P.O. Box 057394
West Palm Beach, FL 33405

Sexual Disorders

Sexual Addicts Anonymous
P.O. Box 3038
Minneapolis, MN 55403

CoSA (Co-dependents of
Sexual Addicts)
Twin Cities CoSA
P.O. Box 14537
Minneapolis, MN 55414

Incest

Incest Survivors Anonymous
P.O. Box 5613
Long Beach, CA 90805

Sexual Abuse Anonymous
P.O. Box 80085
Minneapolis, MN 55408

Survivors of Incest Anonymous
P.O. Box 21817
Baltimore, MD 21222

Miscellaneous Self-Help Information

Self-Help Center
1600 Dodge Ave.
Evanston, IL 60201

Obsessive Compulsive
Anonymous
P.O. Box 215
New Hyde Park, NY 11040

Ruth Fishel

For up-to-date information on Ruth Fishel's workshops, seminars, conferences and tapes or to be on her mailing list, write to:

Ruth Fishel
Spirithaven
1600 Falmouth Road
Suite 175-1980
Centerville, MA 02632
or call: 1-(508)-778-2208 or 1-(508)-778-1226

The following tapes are now available:

You Cannot Meditate Wrong .... $ 9.00

Time For Joy! $10.00

Transforming Your Past Into Presents
Finding Your Own Special Gifts .... $ 9.00

Guided Exercises For Deepening Your
Meditation Experience .... $ 9.00

The Journey Within .... $ 9.00

Discovering Your Source Of Peace With
The Powerful Tool Of Noting .... $ 9.00

NOTES

Chapter 2: Stress

1. Pelletier, Kenneth R. **Mind as Healer, Mind as Slayer.** Dell Publishing, Inc., 1 Dag Hammarskjold Plaza, New York, 10017, 1977. Pages 69-70.
2. Ibid.
3. Borysenko, Ph.D., Joan. **Minding the Body, Mending the Mind.** Addison-Wesley Publishing, 1987. Page 14.
4. Bradshaw, John. **Healing The Shame That Binds You,** Health Communications, Deerfield Beach, FL, 1989. Page 73.
5. Ibid. Page 82.
6. Miller, Alice. **The Drama of the Gifted Child.** Basic Books, 1981. Miller gave credit to Winnicott for this statement. Page 20.
7. Ibid. Page 21.
8. Kritsberg, Wayne. Summarized from **The Adult Children Of Alcoholics Syndrome** by Health Communications, Pompano Beach, FL, 1985.
9. Ibid.
10. Chapter 7.
11. Whitfield, Charles, M.D. **Healing The Child Within.** Health Communications, Pompano Beach, FL, 1987. Page 58.

12. Mooney, Samatha. **A Snowflake In My Hand.** Page 149.

13. Humphrey, Lloyd F. From "Addiction, Recognizing And PSTD, Treating Vietnam Vets," an article in *Alcoholism and Addiction Magazine,* Sept.-Oct., 1988.

Chapter 3: Introducing Endorphins

1. Robert Orbstein and David Sobel. **The Healing Brain.** The Institute For The Study of Human Knowledge, Simon and Schuster, Rockefeller Center, 1230 Avenue of the Americas, New York, NY 10020, 1987. Pages 88-89.

2. Ibid. Page 94.

3. Pelletier. Page 62.

4. Siegal, Bernie, M.D. **Peace, Love and Healing.** Harper & Row, New York, NY, 1989.

5. Ibid.

6. Benson, Herbert, M.D. **Your Maximum Mind.** Avon Books, a division of Hearst Corporation, New York, NY, 1987.

7. Ibid. Pages 93-94.

8. Justice, Blair. **Who Gets Sick? Thinking and Health.** Peak Press, Houston, TX, 1987. Pages 120-121.

9. Ornstein, Robert and Sobel, David. Page 94.

10. Seigal, Bernie, M.D. Page 14.

11. Ibid. Page 15.

12. Martin M. Rossman, M.D. "The Healing Power of Imagery." Article in *New Age Journal.* March/April, 1988.

13. Fox, Arnold, M.D. and Fox, Barry. **Wake Up! You're Alive.** Health Communications, Deerfield Beach, FL, 1988. Page 32.

14. Borysenko, Joan. **Minding The Body, Mending The Mind.** Page 13.

15. Siegal. Page 25.

16. Ibid. Page 38.

17. Cohen, Sydney, M.D. **The Chemical Brain,** Care Institute, CompCare Publishers, 2415 Annapolis Lane, Minneapolis, MN 55441, 1988. Pages 29-31.

18. Justice. Page 242.

19. Ibid. Page 103.
20. Cohen, Sydney, M.D. Page 25.
21. Justice, Blaire. Page 246.
22. Tony A., **The Laundry List.** Health Communications, 1991.
23. Pelletier. Page 4.
24. Ibid. Page 5.
25. Sidney Cohen, M.D., Preface. (Italics and caps emphasis added.)

Chapter 4: Finding Relief

1. Justice. Page 109.
2. Talbott, T. Douglas, M.D., Keynote Address, "Eating Disorders and Other Addictions, A Holistic Disease," U.S. Journal, Inc., Eating Disorders Conference, Atlanta, GA, 1988. Quoted by Kay Sheppard. **Food Addiction.** Health Communications, Deerfield Beach, FL, 1989. Page 38.
3. William, Duffy. **Sugar Blues.** Warner Books, New York, NY, 1976. Page 22. Quoted by Kay Sheppard. **Food Addiction.** Health Communications, Deerfield Beach, FL, 1989. Pages 47-48.
4. Nakken. Page 55.
5. Pelletier. Page 61.

Chapter 5: Addictions And Compulsions

1. Cohen. Page 98.
2. Craig Nakken. **The Addictive Personality: Roots, Ritual and Recovery.** Hazelden Foundation, 1988.
3. Ibid. Page 4.
4. Ibid. Page 6.
5. Ibid. Page 42.
6. Ibid. Page 31.
7. Ibid. Page 11.
8. Ibid. Page 44.
9. Cermak, Timmen L., M.D. **Diagnosing and Treating Co-Dependence.** Johnson Insitute, 510 First Avenue North, Minneapolis, MN 55403, 1986. Pages 27-28.

10. Nakken. Page 42.

11. Carnes, Pat. **Out Of The Shadows.** CompCare, 1983. Page 9.

12. Ibid. Page 10.

13. Benson. Page 8.

Chapter 6: The Heroine's And Hero's Journey

1. Fishel, Ruth, **Time For Joy.** Health Communications, Deerfield Beach, Florida, 1988. January 1st.
2. Johnson, Robert. **We: Understanding the Psychology of Love.** Harper & Row, 1983. Page 2.
3. Campbell, Joseph, **The Hero With A Thousand Faces.** World Publishing, New York, NY, 1971. Page 3.
4. Ibid. Page 11.
5. **A Course In Miracles.** (Manual For Teachers). The Foundation for Inner Peace, Tiburon, CA 94920, 1975. Pages 8-10.
6. May, Robert. **Physicans Of The Soul.** Crossroads, 575 Lexington Avenue, New York, NY, 1982.

Chapter 7: The Hundredth Monkey Syndrome

1. Keyes, Ken, Jr. **The Hundredth Monkey.** Vision Books, 790 Commercial Avenue, Coos Bay, Oregon 97420. This book is not copyrighted. Ken Keyes asks that we reproduce it and distribute it in as many languages as possible, to as many people as possible.

Chapter 8: The 12-Step Movement

1. Alcoholics Anonymous, known as **"The Big Book."** Alcoholics Anonymous World Services, New York, NY, 1939. Page 14.

Chapter 9: The Power Of Recovery

1. Justice. Page 18.
2. Ibid. Page 23.
3. Ibid. Page 15.
4. Ibid. Page 245.
5. Funk and Wagnalls Standard College Dictionary. Funk and Wagnalls Publishing Company, 1974.

6. Justice. Page 119.
7. Siegal. Page 92-93.
8. Justice. Page 54.
9. Martin M. Rossman, M.D. "The Healing Power of Imagery." Article in *New Age Journal*, March/April, 1988.
10. Justice. Page 15.
11. Ibid.
12. Ibid. Page 32.
13. Ibid. Page 122.
14. Ornstein and Sobel. Page 92.
15. Ibid. Page 44.
16. Ibid. Page 12.

Chapter 11: Breaking The Chains Of Our Reactions

1. Hart, William, **The Art of Living: Vispassana Meditation as taught by S.N. Goenka.** Harper & Row, San Francisco, 1987. Page 27.
2. Wilson, Bill. **Twelve Steps and Twelve Traditions.** Alcoholics Anonymous World Services, Box 459, Grand Central Station, New York, NY, 1952. Page 88.
3. Hanh, Thich Nhat. **The Sun in My Heart.** Parallax Press, Berkeley, CA, 1988.
4. Kornfield, Jack. **Seeking the Heart of Wisdom.** Shambhala, 1987. Page 33.
5. Hart. Page 33.
6. This information comes from the audio tape: **Karma** by Joseph Goldstein, and the books, **Seeking the Heart of Wisdom** by Joseph Goldstein and **The Art of Living: Vispassana Meditation as taught by S.N. Goenka** by William Hart.
7. From an article from *Inquiring Mind*, Fall, 1989, by Sharon Salzberg.
8. Goldstein, Joseph. **Karma** tape.

Chapter 14: The Healing Power Of Meditation

1. Siegal. Page 2.
2. Benson. **The Relaxation Response.** Page 320.

3. Borysenko, Joan. **Minding The Body, Mending The Mind.**
4. Siegal. Page 35.
5. Ibid. Page 38.
6. Benson. Page 320.
7. Ibid. Page 9.
8. Bedford Combs discussed this at a U.S. Journal Conference in Charlotte, NC, in May 1990.
9. Martin M. Rossman, M.D., "The Healing Power of Imagery." Article in *New Age Journal*, March/April, 1988.
10. **Twelve Steps and Twelve Traditions,** by the A.A. Grapevine, Inc., 1952 and Alcoholics Anonymous Publishing now known as Alcohol Anonymous World Service, Box 459, Grand Central Station, Inc., New York, NY 10163.
11. Fishel, Ruth, revised and updated. Originally printed in **The Journey Within: A Spiritual Path to Recovery.**
12. Thich Nhat Hanh.
13. Wilson, Bill. Step Eleven.
14. Wilson, Bill. Step Ten.
15. Ibid.
16. I have taken the liberty of changing "He" to "God" to reflect universality and erase sex pronouns in "The Twelve Steps of Recovery."
17. Wilson, Bill. Contents, Pages 5-9.
18. Goldstein.

Chapter 16: Basic Sitting Meditation Instructions

1. Fishel, Ruth, revised and updated. The Basic Meditation Instructions were originally printed in **The Journey Within: A Spiritual Path to Recovery.** The following meditations and guided imageries found in this chapter of **Healing Energy: The Power of Recovery** have been revised: Basic Meditation, page 231; Special symbols, page 236; Inner Sanctuary Meditation, page 238; Inner Guide Meditation, page 231.
2. Wilson. Step Eleven.
3. Insight Meditation Society, Barre, MA.

Recommended Reading List

Alcoholics Anonymous. Alcoholics Anonymous World Service, Box 459, Grand Central Station, New York, NY 10163, 1939.

Being Peace. Thich Nhat Hanh. Parallax Press, P.O. Box 7355, Berkeley, CA 94707, 1987.

Beyond Co-dependency. Melody Beattie. Hazelden Foundation, Harper and Row Publishers, 10 East 53rd St., NY, NY 10022, 1989.

Course In Miracles. The Foundation for Inner Peace, P.O. Box 635, Tiburton, CA 94920, 1975.

Diagnosing And Treating Co-dependence. Timmen L. Cermak. Johnson Institute Books, 510 First Avenue North, Minneapolis, MN 55403, 1986.

Heal Your Self-Esteem: Recovery From Addictive Thinking. Bryan Robinson. Health Communications, Deerfield Beach, FL 33442, 1991.

Healing The Child Within. Charles L. Whitfield, M.D. Health Communications, Pompano Beach, FL 33442, 1987.

Healing The Shame That Binds You. John Bradshaw. Health Communications, Deerfield Beach, FL 33442, 1988.

Healing Yourself. Martin L. Rossman. Walker Publishing, NY, 1987.

Learning To Live In The Now. Ruth Fishel. Health Communications, Pompano Beach, FL 33442, 1988.

Mind As Healer, Mind As Slayer. Kenneth R. Pelletier. Dell, New York, NY 10017, 1977.

Minding The Body, Mending The Mind. Joan Borysenko. Addison-Wesley NY, 1987.

Out Of The Shadow. Pat Carnes. CompCare Publications, MN 55441, 1983.

Peace, Love And Healing. Bernie S. Siegal. Harper and Row, New York, NY 10022, 1989.

Physicians Of The Soul. Robert May. Crossroad Publishing, NY, NY 10022, 1982.

Seeking The Heart Of Wisdom. Joseph Goldstein and Jack Kornfield. Shambala Publications, Boston, MA 02115, 1987.

Sexual Recovery. Gina Ogden. Health Communciations, Deerfield Beach, FL 33442, 1990.

Sun In My Heart. Thich Nhat Hanh. Parallax Press. Berkeley, CA 94707, 1988.

The Addictive Personality: Roots, Ritual and Recovery. Craig Nakken. Hazelden Foundation, Center City, MN 55012-0176, 1988.

The Chemical Brain. Sydney Cohen. CompCare Publishers, Minneapolis, MN 55441, 1988.

The Drama Of The Gifted Child. Alice Miller. Basic Books, NY, 1981.

The Healing Brain. Robert Ornstein and David Sobel. Simon and Schuster, NY, NY 10020, 1987.

The Hero With A Thousand Faces. Joseph Campbell. World Publishing, New York, 1971.

The Hundredth Monkey. Ken Keyes, Jr. Vision Books, Coos Bay, OR 97420, 1986.

The Journey Within. Ruth Fishel. Health Communications, Pompano Beach, FL 33442, 1987.

Karuna, A Journal of Buddhist Meditation, Karuna Meditation Society, P.O. Box 24468, Station C, Vancouver, B.C. V5T 4M5.

The Miracle Of Mindfulness. Thich Nhat Hanh. Beacon Press, Boston, MA., 1976.

The Path Of Action. Jack Schwartz. E.P. Dutton, New York, 1977.

The Adult Children Of Alcoholics Syndrome. Wayne Kritsberg. Health Communications, Pompano Beach, FL 33442, 1985.

Time For Joy. Ruth Fishel. Health Communications, Pompano Beach, FL 33442, 1988.

Transforming The Co-dependent Woman. Sandra Bierig. Health Communications, Deerfield Beach, FL 33442, 1991.

Twelve Steps And Twelve Traditions. Alcoholics Anonymous World Services, New York, NY 10163, 1952.

Vipassana Meditation as taught by S.N. Goenka and written by William Hart, Harper and Row, San Francisco, CA 1987.

Voices Of Our Ancestors. Dhyani Ywahoo. Shambala Publications, Boston, MA 02115, 1987.

Wake Up! You're Alive. Arnold Fox, M.D. and Barry Fox. Health Communications, Deerfield Beach, FL 33442, 1988.

Your Maximum Mind. Dr. Herbert Benson. Avon Books, NY, NY 10016, 1986.

Zen Mind, Beginner's Mind. Shunryu Suzuki. John Weatherhill, Inc., 7-6-13 Roppongi, Minato-ku, Tokyo 106.

For further up-to-date information on retreats and articles on Vipassana Meditation write to:

The Inquiring Mind: A Semi-Annual Journal of the Vipassana Community, P.O. Box 9999, North Berkeley Station, Berkeley, CA 94709.

For up-to-date information on Ruth Fishel's workshops, seminars, conferences and tapes or to be on her mailing list, write to:

Ruth Fishel
Spirithaven
1600 Falmouth Road
Suite 175-1980
Centerville, MA 02632
or call: 1-(508)-778-2208 or 1-(508)-778-1226

Daily Affirmation Books from . . .
Health Communications

GENTLE REMINDERS FOR CO-DEPENDENTS: Daily Affirmations
Mitzi Chandler

With insight and humor, Mitzi Chandler takes the co-dependent and the adult child through the year. Gentle Reminders is for those in recovery who seek to enjoy the miracle each day brings.

ISBN 1-55874-020-1 **$6.95**

TIME FOR JOY: Daily Affirmations
Ruth Fishel

With quotations, thoughts and healing energizing affirmations these daily messages address the fears and imperfections of being human, guiding us through self-acceptance to a tangible peace and the place within where there is *time for joy.*

ISBN 0-932194-82-6 **$6.95**

AFFIRMATIONS FOR THE INNER CHILD
Rokelle Lerner

This book contains powerful messages and helpful suggestions aimed at adults who have unfinished childhood issues. By reading it daily we can end the cycle of suffering and move from pain into recovery.

ISBN 1-55874-045-6 **$6.95**

DAILY AFFIRMATIONS: For Adult Children of Alcoholics
Rokelle Lerner

Affirmations are a way to discover personal awareness, growth and spiritual potential, and self-regard. Reading this book gives us an opportunity to nurture ourselves, learn who we are and what we want to become.

ISBN 0-932194-47-3
(Little Red Book) **$6.95**
(New Cover Edition) **$6.95**

SOOTHING MOMENTS: Daily Meditations For Fast-Track Living
Bryan E. Robinson, Ph.D.

This is designed for those leading fast-paced and high-pressured lives who need time out each day to bring self-renewal, joy and serenity into their lives.

ISBN 1-55874-075-9 **$6.95**

3201 S.W. 15th Street,
Deerfield Beach, FL 33442-8190
1-800-851-9100